Brehe's GRAMMAR *Anatomy*

STEVEN BREHE

Blue Ridge | Cumming | Dahlonega | Gainesville | Oconee

Brehe's Grammar Anatomy is licensed under a Creative Commons Attribution-ShareAlike 4.0 International License.

This license allows you to remix, tweak, and build upon this work, even commercially, as long as you credit this original source for the creation and license the new creation under identical terms.

If you reuse this content elsewhere, in order to comply with the attribution requirements of the license please attribute the original source to the University System of Georgia.

NOTE: The above copyright license which University System of Georgia uses for their original content does not extend to or include content which was accessed and incorporated, and which is licensed under various other CC Licenses, such as ND licenses. Nor does it extend to or include any Special Permissions which were granted to us by the rightsholders for our use of their content.

Image Disclaimer: All images and figures in this book are believed to be (after a reasonable investigation) either public domain or carry a compatible Creative Commons license. If you are the copyright owner of images in this book and you have not authorized the use of your work under these terms, please contact the University of North Georgia Press at ungpress@ung.edu to have the content removed.

ISBN: 978-1-940771-49-6

Produced by:
University System of Georgia

Published by:
University of North Georgia Press
Dahlonega, Georgia

Cover Design and Layout Design:
Corey Parson

For more information, please visit http://ung.edu/university-press
Or email ungpress@ung.edu

Table of Contents

	Introduction: Grammar? What Grammar?	v
1	Together Forever: Subjects and Predicates	1
2	The Indispensables: Nouns and Verbs	6
3	Get Tense: Verb Tense, Principal Parts, and Irregular Verbs	16
4	Tall, Dark, and Wordsome: Adjectives	30
5	Inevitably, Adverbs	41
6	Among the Prepositions	52
7	You and I and the Personal Pronouns	65
8	You Did *What*? Verbs and Their Complements	81
9	All Together Now: Conjunctions, Compounds, and Subordinate Clauses	91
10	Sentencing Guidelines: Building Sentences with Clauses	113
11	Relative Clauses, Which We Need	126
12	I Know That You Know What They Are: Nominal Clauses	140
13	They're *So* Dependent: Distinguishing Dependent Clauses	147

14	What, *More*? Verbs and Voice, Infinitives, and Passive Complements	158
15	They're *So* Common: More on Nouns	168
16	Zowie! Interjections and the Eight Parts of Speech	179
17	Those Verbing Verbals: Gerunds and Participles	185
18	To Boldly Verb: Infinitives	197
19	What's *That*? More Pronouns	212
20	Many Things (But no Cabbages or Kings)	221
21	Keeping Those Little Puncs in Line: A Brief Review of Punctuation	233
	Answer Key	251
	Glossary	316
	Index	338

Introduction

Grammar? What Grammar?

When we speak or write, or listen or read, we create sentences with words and phrases. **Grammar** is the system of rules that guide us as we make and comprehend the sentences of others. All languages have some kind of grammar.

When we use the word *grammar* in the sense discussed here, that "system of rules" does not necessarily include rules like "Never end a sentence with a preposition," or "Don't dangle your participle around here, bub." That kind of rule may often be helpful, but it's not what this book is generally about.

So what rules are we talking about here? To begin with an example, we might say this:

On Tuesday, Devlin caught Alicia in the wine cellar.

Or I could say this:

On Tuesday, Alicia caught Devlin in the wine cellar.

(On Tuesday, Alicia and Devlin had more fun than I've had all year.)

But the point is this: Those two sentences contain exactly the same words. The only difference is the placement of *Devlin* and

Alicia, and that difference alters the meaning of the sentence considerably.

Sometimes we can move words around without changing the meaning at all:

<u>Alicia</u> and <u>Devlin</u> are characters in Hitchcock's film *Notorious*.
<u>Devlin</u> and <u>Alicia</u> are characters in Hitchcock's film *Notorious*.

If we put some words in a certain order, it makes one meaning, and we change the meaning when we rearrange certain words. Other changes don't alter the meaning at all. Those are some of the things we mean by the rules of grammar: Certain word orders and changes are meaningful in certain ways and others aren't.

Here's another example. Suppose we alter the sentence this way:

Tuesday on caught cellar Alicia Devlin wine the in.

(If you talk like that, you're spending too much time in the wine cellar.)

In this example, we've used the same words but arranged them haphazardly, and with that order, the words make no meaning at all. That's what happens when you break too many grammar rules.

There are still other kinds of rules:

<u>He</u> caught <u>her</u> in the wine cellar.
<u>She</u> caught <u>him</u> in the wine cellar.

(Just where is this wine cellar and *how* do I get there?)

We know, as speakers of English, that *he* and *him* both refer to Devlin, and *she* and *her* refer to Alicia. So why do we have to use different words? Why not use *he* and *she* in both sentences, and forget about *him* and *her*?

We can't, because the rules of English say so: We have to use one form—one **inflection**—of *he* and *she* if they appear before *caught,* and another inflection (*him* and *her*) if they appear after *caught.*

If you've spoken English all your life, you already know that rule, even if no one ever taught it to you. You learned it intuitively when you were very young—that is, you learned it simply by listening to other English speakers—and now you seldom have to stop and think about when to use *he* and when to use *him.*

But a speaker who is just learning English may have to study and practice rules like that. At this point, we should stress that, *for beginning students of English as a second language,* there are definitely more helpful books than this one. For you, this book may not be the best starting place.

Here we will assume that our reader has an intuitive understanding of many such rules of English. We'll often refer to them, because they're helpful in learning about other matters of English grammar.

BUT WHY? WHY?

Understanding the basics of English grammar is helpful whenever we study language. When we're learning to become better writers, for instance, we have to discuss language, and that requires some knowledge of the terms and concepts of sentence structure—that is, of grammar.

For example, we may discuss improving something we wrote by rewriting a passive sentence as an active sentence. But discussing that improvement—and making it—means we need to recognize a **passive verb** and know how to change it into an **active verb**, and then make all the related changes in the sentence.

The terms and concepts you learn in English grammar apply to other languages, too. Many of the grammatical concepts of English apply to other European languages, and some apply to non-European languages as well. That means that English speakers can use grammatical terms and concepts they already know to help them learn a new language. For example, it's easier for English speakers to learn about **direct** and **indirect objects** in German if they already understand these concepts in English.

Any time we want to learn about language or discuss it, basic grammatical terms and concepts are likely to be useful. We encounter those terms and concepts in dictionaries and other reference works; we encounter them in books on linguistics and psychology.

So why study grammar? To become a better writer? To learn a new language? To study linguistics? To become an English teacher? To use a dictionary more effectively? If you want to do any of these things, you'll find a basic knowledge of grammar helpful.

SENTENCING GUIDELINES

The **simple declarative sentence** is the usual basis of all grammatical study. Other kinds of sentences are important, but we begin with declaratives.

A **declarative sentence** doesn't ask a question or give an order. It simply makes a statement, an assertion. All of the following sentences are examples of declarative sentences:

Mr. Morton lives in our neighborhood.
Mr. Morton is a pest.
I like Mr. Morton.
High Street takes you out to the city park.
The old train station stands on Front Street, by the river.

In the chapters that follow, we'll primarily focus on declarative sentences.

But what is a **sentence**? One common definition—one you may have heard before—goes like this:

A sentence is a unit of language that contains a **subject** and a **predicate** and expresses a complete idea.

Audiences of professional linguists, when presented with this definition, hiss, boo, and throw vine-ripened tomatoes. (They're an unruly lot.) They raise plenty of objections about it too, especially concerning the vague notion of "a complete idea." But we often encounter this definition in introductory grammar courses because it doesn't require students to know many grammatical terms or concepts. For the time being, we'll settle for this familiar definition. But hold your fire; we'll return to the task of defining the sentence later, after we've learned a bit more. (And we will explain subjects and predicates in the first chapter.)

WHAT KIND OF GRAMMAR?

There are various approaches to grammar. For example, you may have heard of the approach called *generative grammar* (or sometimes *transformational-generative grammar*), associated with the linguist Noam Chomsky. That is an important and influential approach to language, but not one that we'll discuss in this course. You may encounter it, however, in books on linguistics, where you'll also encounter many of the terms discussed here.

The approach in this book is sometimes called *traditional grammar* or *classroom grammar* because it is often used in English and modern language classrooms, where it has long been taught. (Grammar is always taught long and never short. Suck it up.)

WHAT YOU *SHOULD* DO OR WHAT YOU *DO* DO?

Approaches to grammar can also be classified as *prescriptive* or *descriptive*.

Putting it simply, **prescriptive grammar** tells students how they *should* speak and write to communicate in the *standard dialect* of their language, the variety of English used by educated speakers.

Descriptive grammar describes the ways language is actually used, even by speakers of non-standard dialects. Descriptive grammar seldom makes explicit judgments about what is right or wrong in a sentence.

Like many approaches to grammar, the approach in the following chapters is to some extent a combination of the prescriptive and descriptive. This book *describes* the grammar of Standard American English—the variety educated Americans usually speak and write in professional situations—and so this book implicitly (and sometimes explicitly) *prescribes* standard uses over others. But much of what we'll learn here applies to any variety of English.

Every language has its own internal logic, however inconsistent it may sometimes be. Learn a few premises, usually simple ones, concerning things like word order, or number, **case**, and **tense**, and you'll understand something of the logic of a language, even if you don't yet know all the cases and tenses. You'll see that many features of English grammar are clearly and simply logical. And some aren't. (And some aren't even *trying*.)

HOW MUCH GRAMMAR?

This is an introductory book: It gives you the most basic, the most frequently used terms and concepts of English grammar.

By comparison, *A Comprehensive Grammar of the English Language* (by Quirk, Greenbaum, and others) is 1792 pages long. *The Cambridge Grammar of the English Language* (by Pullum, Huddleston, and others) is 1860 pages long.

This book is nowhere near as complete, or as long. (You're welcome.)

But even a basic book like this one offers challenges. This book contains roughly 200 grammatical terms, some that you may have encountered before, and others that may be new to you. The workings of English (or any other language) is a vast topic. Even an introductory text, if it aims to give you a good start, will cover a good deal of territory. That's why it's important to know about—and use—the resources available in this book.

USING THIS BOOK

One way to get a good grasp of what you learn here is to do the exercises at the end of each chapter and check your work by looking up the answers in the back of this book. If you make mistakes, reexamine the exercises you missed until you understand your mistake. Don't write the answers in your text—that way, you can return to the chapter and use the exercises again for review and practice.

When you don't remember what a particular term means, you can always find out by using the index or by consulting the glossary in the back of the book, which will also refer you to the relevant chapter.

As we'll remind you again and again, having a dictionary handy is important when you're studying English grammar (or any language for that matter). Dictionaries can help you figure out if a particular word is an adverb or a preposition or a conjunction, or the right form of a verb or plural noun.

Good online dictionaries make looking up words fast and easy, and they have the kinds of grammatical information you'll sometimes need. Here are some online dictionaries you could consult:

- www.merriam-webster.com
- www.dictionary.com

- www.ahdictionary.com
  (the online *American Heritage Dictionary*)

The online *Oxford English Dictionary*, the massive historical dictionary, is a wonderful resource, but it may overwhelm you with the sheer quantity and range of its information. We'd recommend that you do *not* refer to it as you begin to learn about grammar. (But it's still fun to browse through.)

And now we'll find out more about those declarative sentences; on to Chapter 1.

1

Together Forever

Subjects and Predicates

We'll begin with **declarative sentences**, sentences that make a statement instead of asking questions or giving orders. All of the examples you'll see in the next several chapters are declarative sentences.

As we begin, it's helpful to know that declarative sentences in English usually follow this basic pattern:

Subject + Predicate

The subject comes first, and the predicate follows—usually.

IT'S *ALL* ABOUT THE SUBJECT

The **subject** is the star, the *prima donna*, of the sentence. It's the part of the sentence that names who or what the sentence is about.

The **predicate** always tells us something about the subject. Usually, the predicate tells us what the subject is doing (or has done), or it describes the subject.

These very simple sentences follow the simple **Subject + Predicate** pattern:

Subject	+	Predicate
Alice		fell.
The cat		smiled.
Carroll		wrote.
Julie		sang.
Fish		swim.
Birds		fly.
Hammerstein		composed.

As these sentences illustrate, the subject and the predicate can each be only one word, so it's possible to write a complete declarative sentence in just two words. (We cheated with *The cat smiled.*) In longer sentences, which we'll see shortly, identifying the subjects and predicates of sentences becomes easy with practice.

THE SIMPLE AND THE COMPLETE

Every simple declarative sentence that we've seen contains a subject and a predicate, and the subject usually appears to the left of the predicate, at the beginning of the sentence or near it.

In these cases, the **complete subject** and the **complete predicate** are each just one word long. There's one exception: *The cat.*

We can add more words to those subjects and predicates. We can add **modifiers**, words that describe the subject and the predicate:

Birds **fly.**
Most **birds** in the United States **fly** well.

In this longer sentence, we call *birds* the **simple subject** and *fly* the **simple predicate**.

We call *Most birds in the United States* the **complete subject**, and we call *fly well* the **complete predicate**. That is, the simple subject and all its modifiers make up the complete subject. And the simple predicate with all its modifiers is the complete predicate. So, in *Birds fly*, the simple subject and the complete subject are identical, and so are the simple and complete predicates.

Here are more examples, with the simple subjects and predicates in boldface:

A beautiful **day** like today	**comes** too seldom.
Mary's **cat**	**ran** away yesterday.

As the examples above show, some modifiers appear immediately before the word they modify: *A, beautiful, Mary's, too*. But some modifiers can appear afterward, too: *like today, seldom, away, yesterday*.

In the next examples, we begin with the sentence *Irises grow*. In each example, the simple subject and predicate are in bold; the complete predicate is underlined; and the rest of the sentence (the part not underlined) is the complete subject:

Irises	**grow**.
Sometimes **irises**	**grow** well near the garage.
In the spring **irises**	**grow** well in our garden.

Here again, some modifiers of *grow* appear immediately before or after the word they modify: *well, near the garage, in our garden*. And some modifiers of the predicate can even appear at some distance from *grow*: *Sometimes, In the spring*.

Here are some more pairs of sentences, with the simple subject and the simple predicate in bold type and the complete predicate underlined:

Many **birds** in the U. S. **fly** south in the winter.
In the winter, many **birds** in the U. S. **fly** south.

Oscar Hammerstein composed rapidly in the winter of 1927.
In the winter of 1927, **Oscar Hammerstein composed** rapidly.

As you see in the second sentence of each pair, parts of the complete predicate can appear before the subject. This is a common sentence pattern, and we'll have more to say about it in later chapters.

TRANSPOSED ORDER

In some sentences, it's possible to put the entire predicate before the subject; this is called **transposed order** (also known as *inverted order*). In the following sentences, the simple subjects and predicates are in bold type, and the complete predicate is underlined:

<u>Softly **fell**</u> the **rain**.
<u>Gently **came**</u> the **dawn**.
<u>Into the quiet village **roared**</u> the **steam locomotive**.

Use transposed order with restraint, or it can become just a way of showing off with words.

In the next few chapters, we'll learn more about subjects, predicates, and modifiers.

EXERCISES

Answers to these exercises are in the back of the book. After you answer one set, check your answers before you go on—sometimes the answers will help you with the next set.

1a. Write the definitions of the simple subject and the simple predicate.

1b. In the following sentences, identify the simple subject and the simple predicate. To help you, the complete predicate is <u>underlined</u>.

1. Rain <u>falls</u>.
2. Edward <u>knocked at the door</u>.
3. <u>In the morning</u>, the family <u>ate on the porch</u>.
4. <u>In the morning</u>, pancakes <u>seemed like a good idea</u>.
5. <u>Into the night, into the darkness, recklessly rode</u> Rudolpho.

1c. You'll get no help with these! Once again, identify the simple subject and the simple predicate. Then identify the complete subject and the complete predicate.

1. Wendell behaved politely.
2. Tonight that nice family ate on the porch again.
3. Backward ran sentences. [Modified from Wolcott Gibbs.]
4. In the spring, the calla lilies were in bloom again.
5. This morning Rudolpho was waiting on the porch for breakfast.

The Indispensables
Nouns and Verbs

Nouns and verbs are two of the most basic and important concepts in grammar.

SUBJECTS AND NOUNS

In the sentences we've seen, the simple subjects are all **nouns**. This traditional definition of nouns will serve our purpose:

A **noun** is a word that names a person, place, thing, or idea.

Nouns name persons: man, woman, child, children, student, teacher, Mr. Morton, Oscar Hammerstein.
They name places: kitchen, home, Main Street, St. Louis, Missouri, U.S.A., North America, Earth, solar system, the Milky Way.
They name things: pen, ink, paper, printing press, telegraph, linotype, typewriter, computer, smart phone, internet.
Nouns also name ideas—that, is, abstractions: science, mathematics, truth, beauty, democracy, Platonism, Catholicism, Calvinism.
Most simple subjects are nouns.

PREDICATES AND VERBS

In any sentence, the simple predicate is a **verb**—an indispensable part of English sentences. For our purposes, this definition will do:

A **verb** is a word or group of words that names an action or indicates a state of being.

There are two general classes of verb. One kind of verb—an **action verb**—names actions:

Hammerstein <u>composed</u>.
George <u>loves</u> Ethel.
Pearl <u>painted</u> Mr. Morton's porch.

Another kind of verb names "states of being"—that is, they appear in predicates that describe the subject. These verbs are called **linking verbs**.

Gershwin <u>was</u> a composer.
George <u>became</u> thoughtful.
Pearl <u>seems</u> busy.

There are thousands of verbs in English, and the great majority of them are action verbs: *sit, stand, hit, run, hide, seek, say, sing, create, declare, denounce, pontificate, shout, cry, laugh,* and all the rest.

Some action verbs name activities that are not actions in the usual sense: *have, pause, think, consider, wait.*

There are relatively few linking verbs in English. The most common are the eight forms of the verb *be*:

be	are
been	is
being	was
am	were

It's helpful to commit all the forms of *be* to memory, because you'll need to recognize them again and again in this book and in other works about English grammar.

Here are some of the other linking verbs: *seem, become, remain.* Many linking verbs are related to our senses: *look, feel, smell, sound, taste, appear*:

Bill <u>looked</u> angry.
Bill <u>sounded</u> angry.
Bill <u>felt</u> angry.
The kitchen <u>smelled</u> wonderful.
The soup <u>tasted</u> good.

The examples of linking verbs may seem confusing because some verbs can be used as action verbs (*Bob appeared suddenly*) or as linking verbs (*Bob appeared ill*).

To clarify the differences, consider the following pairs of sentences. The first sentence in each pair contains a linking verb; the second contains an action verb:

Frank <u>felt</u> well.
Frank <u>felt</u> the cold air.

Marsha <u>looked</u> wonderful.
Marsha <u>looked</u> out the window.

The tomatoes <u>tasted</u> sweet.
We <u>tasted</u> the tomatoes.

Ed <u>remained</u> stubborn.
Ed <u>remained</u> in his room.

In each pair, the first sentence with the linking verb describes the subject in some way. The second sentence with the action verb tells us what the subject did. Many of the words that follow the verbs are not modifiers but other kinds of words that we'll learn about soon.

AUXILIARY VERBS AND MAIN VERBS

Compare the verbs in these pairs of sentences:

Mr. Morton <u>broke</u> the vase.
Mr. Morton <u>has broken</u> another vase.

Jeff <u>sang</u> an old Irish song.
Jeff <u>should have sung</u> an old Lithuanian song.

Martha <u>won</u> the race.
Martha <u>should have been winning</u> all along.

In the second sentence of each pair, the simple predicate consists of more than one verb. In any sentence, the verb can be one to four words long:

Mr. Morton <u>broke</u> the vase.
Mr. Morton <u>has broken</u> another vase.
Mr. Morton <u>has been breaking</u> vases all afternoon.
Mr. Morton <u>should</u> not <u>have been juggling</u> vases.

In any sentence with two or more words in the verb, the rightmost verb is called the **main verb**. In the four sentences just above, *broke, broken, breaking,* and *juggling* are the main verbs.

All the other words in the underlined verb are **auxiliary verbs** (sometimes called *helping verbs*). Together the auxiliary verbs and the main verb make the simple predicate, which is the entire verb of the sentence. The simple predicate can be one to four words long and includes only the main verb (which is always present) and its auxiliary verbs (if any).

It is the main verb that determines if the simple predicate is an action verb or linking verb.

Here's a list of the auxiliary verbs in English:

am	have	do	can	may
are	has	does	could	might
is	had	did	shall	must
was			should	
were			will	
be			would	
been				
being				

There are eight forms of *be*, three forms of *have*, three forms of *do*, three rhyming pairs (*can/could; shall/should; will/would*), and three *m-* verbs. Sometimes words like *ought to* and *have to* are included among the auxiliaries. We'll discuss those later in Chapter 20.

You don't have to memorize the entire list, but you should refer to it often until you can recognize auxiliary verbs when you see them. You should also learn all the forms of the verb *be* in the first column.

Remember that auxiliary verbs always come before the main verb. Also notice that some auxiliaries can be used as main verbs:

Rhianna was planning the party.   [*Was* is the auxiliary.]
Rhianna was early.   [*Was* is the main verb.]

The Browns <u>have purchased</u> the gift.   [*Have* is the auxiliary.]
The Browns <u>have</u> the receipt.   [*Have* is the main verb.]

The Greens <u>do like</u> reading.   [*Do* is the auxiliary.]
The Greens <u>do</u> the dishes every day.   [*Do* is the main verb.]

Still other auxiliaries in the list are used only as auxiliaries, as in these examples:

Al <u>can</u> go.   Hal <u>may</u> go.
Al <u>could</u> go.   Hal <u>might</u> tango.
Al <u>will</u> go.   No, Hal <u>must</u> go.
Al <u>would</u> go.
Al <u>shall</u> go.
Al <u>should</u> just go.

Notice that many of the auxiliaries are present or past forms: *Could, should,* and *would* are the past forms of *can, shall,* and *will*. We see this usage in sentences like this:

My uncle <u>can</u> play the harmonica well.
My late uncle <u>could</u> play the harmonica well.

In Chapter 20, we'll see some of these same words used as **modal auxiliaries**, which often indicate a *future* possible action:

If you practiced, you <u>could</u> play the harmonica well.

The verb *do* is also worth a bit of attention, because we use it in English as an auxiliary for questions and for emphasis:

<u>Does</u> Paula write well?   <u>Did</u> Paula arrive early?
Yes, Paula <u>does</u> write well.   Yes, Paula <u>did</u> arrive early.

When you're learning another language and want to translate an English sentence that uses *do* for a question or for emphasis, you'll probably find that other languages don't use their equivalent of *do* in this way.

Sometimes the complete verb is interrupted by another word or two. These usually appear after the first auxiliary verb:

Mr. Morton <u>has</u> actually <u>broken</u> another vase.
Mr. Morton <u>should</u> probably not <u>have been juggling</u> vases.
We <u>will</u> definitely not <u>be inviting</u> Mr. Morton back.

The words that interrupt the verb are **adverbs**, which we'll learn about shortly.

POINTS FOR WRITERS

1. Subject-verb agreement.

One of the most basic features of English is that the form of the verb sometimes changes to match a change in the subject. If the subject is singular, the verb will have one form:

Pam <u>sings</u>.
Mom <u>drives</u>.
Ed <u>listens</u>.

But if the subject is plural, the verb may take another form:

Pam and Jim <u>sing</u>.
Mom and Dad <u>drive</u>.
Ed and Alice <u>listen</u>.

The change in the verb for singular and plural subjects is called **subject-verb agreement**. The verb must *agree* with the subject.

Agreement doesn't make the verb change in every case. For instance, the verb doesn't change form when the sentence is about something that happened in the past:

Pam <u>sang</u>.
Pam and Jim <u>sang</u>.

Mom <u>drove</u>.
Mom and Dad <u>drove</u>.

Ed <u>listened</u>.
Ed and Alice <u>listened</u>.

If you've spoken English since you were young, you probably make the verb agree without even being aware of it because it's second nature to you. We'll look more closely at agreement in Chapter 9.

2. May *and* can.

As you may already know, there is an important difference between the auxiliary verbs *may* and *can*. *May* is often used to ask or grant permission or to indicate possibility:

<u>May</u> Jim leave the room?
Yes, Jim <u>may</u>.
Jim <u>may</u> leave, but he hasn't decided.

Can is used to discuss ability:

<u>Can</u> Jim reach the top shelf?
I think he <u>can</u>.

In everyday conversation, we often confuse *can* and *may*, and it seldom matters because our listeners can understand us in the immediate context. In careful writing, the distinction may be important, and failing to observe it is sometimes seen as a mark of a careless writer.

EXERCISES

2a. In the sentences below, underline the complete predicates. Then enclose the simple subjects and simple predicates in brackets, like this:

[Sue] [did call] yesterday.

1. The family was having coffee.

2. The family was content.

3. Without warning, John entered the room.

4. John made an announcement.

5. The vases are gone.

6. The family became furious.

7. Mr. Morton had struck again.

8. Mr. Morton had some nerve.

9. Someday that man will regret his actions.

10. Mr. Morton's reputation has been damaged by these allegations.

11. Everywhere people are hiding their vases.

12. Mr. Morton seems a little strange.

2b. Now, in the sentences that you just examined, identify action verbs (with *A*) and linking verbs (with *L*), as in this example:

[Sue] [did call] yesterday. (A)

2c. Finally, identify the auxiliary verbs and the main verb in each sentence you've examined. Remember, if there's only one verb, it must be the main verb.

3 Get Tense

Verb Tense, Principal Parts, and Irregular Verbs

This chapter is long, but be at ease, Louise. Much of this chapter consists of examples that illustrate the ideas discussed here. Most of it is *not* difficult.

There's a good deal to know about verbs, including the matters of verb **tenses** and the related notions of the **principal parts** of verbs and the **regular** and **irregular verbs**.

The good news is that you know much of this already. You've used the tenses and principal parts ever since you learned to talk. What may be new to you here are the terms that we apply to them and the way we organize them. So relax, Max.

THE TENSES

Tense? We don't mean over-caffeinated verbs. We mean that, in the right context, verbs communicate that an action took place in the present, past, or future.

English has four sets of tenses, and each set contains a present, a past, and a future tense, each with its own distinctions in reference to time. Here we'll examine briefly all four sets:

The **simple tenses**: present, past, and future.
The **perfect tenses**: present, past, and future.

The **simple progressive tenses**: present, past, and future.
The **perfect progressive tenses**: present, past, and future.

THE SIMPLE TENSES

These are the tenses we use most often:

SIMPLE PRESENT:	Today I <u>phone</u> my mother.
SIMPLE PAST:	Yesterday I <u>phoned</u> my mother.
SIMPLE FUTURE:	Tomorrow I <u>will phone</u> my mother.

Notice that we seldom use the simple present in a sentence like "Today I phone my mother." Instead, we use the simple past:

Today I phoned my mother.

Or we use the simple future,

Today I will phone my mother.

Or we use a tense that we'll examine in a moment, the present progressive tense:

I'm phoning my mother right now.

But we'll continue to use this somewhat unusual form in our examples of the simple present.

Here are more examples of the simple tenses:

SIMPLE PRESENT:	Today I <u>talk</u>.
SIMPLE PAST:	Yesterday I <u>talked</u>.
SIMPLE FUTURE:	Tomorrow I <u>will talk</u>.

SIMPLE PRESENT:	Today I <u>walk</u>.
SIMPLE PAST:	Yesterday I <u>walked</u>.
SIMPLE FUTURE:	Tomorrow I <u>will walk</u>.
SIMPLE PRESENT:	Today I <u>build</u>.
SIMPLE PAST:	Yesterday I <u>built</u>.
SIMPLE FUTURE:	Tomorrow I <u>will build</u>.

As these examples show, we create the simple present tense by using the simplest possible form of a verb. The simple present ends with *-s* in cases like these: *he phones, he talks, he builds.*

For the great majority of English verbs, we create the simple past tense by adding *-d* (as in *phoned*) or *-ed* (as in *talked, walked,* or *hunted*) to the present form. In a few cases, we make the past by adding *-t* (as in *built*).

With all verbs, we create the simple future tense by adding the auxiliary verb *will* to the simple present form.

THE PERFECT TENSES

The **perfect tenses** are not called perfect because they're flawless. (Only your grammar teacher is flawless.) They are called *perfect* because the perfect tenses describe actions that have already been completed (i.e., perfected) at some point in the past, present, or future.

All the perfect tenses are based on a form of the main verb called the **past participle**, which in most verbs is identical to the form in the simple past tense. (We'll see more of the past participle a bit later.)

Verbs in the present perfect tense always add the auxiliary verb *have* (or *has*) to the past participle form. They refer to actions that were recently completed:

I <u>have called</u> my mother today.
She <u>has called</u> her mother today.

Verbs in the past perfect tense always add the auxiliary *had* to the past participle form. They refer to actions completed at some point in the past:

I had called my mother by noon yesterday.

The future perfect tense, like the simple future tense, always begins with the auxiliary *will,* followed by *have*:

By noon tomorrow I will have called my mother.

Here are some examples:

PRESENT PERFECT: Today I have talked.
PAST PERFECT: As of yesterday, I had talked.
FUTURE PERFECT: By this time tomorrow I will have talked.

PRESENT PERFECT: Today I have walked.
PAST PERFECT: As of yesterday, I had walked.
FUTURE PERFECT: By this time tomorrow I will have walked.

PRESENT PERFECT: Today I have complained.
PAST PERFECT: As of yesterday, I had complained.
FUTURE PERFECT: By this time tomorrow I will have complained.

If you compare the main verbs in these perfect tense sentences with the main verbs in the simple past sentences that we saw earlier, you'll see that they are exactly the same words. This is a point that we'll return to when we discuss regular and irregular verbs.

THE SIMPLE PROGRESSIVE AND PERFECT PROGRESSIVE TENSES

The **simple progressive tenses** refer to actions that have been in progress at a particular point in time. The main verbs in the progressive tenses always end in *-ing*, and they always take an auxiliary verb that is a form of the verb *be*.

The future progressive tense always begins with the auxiliaries *will be*. Here are some examples:

PRESENT PROGRESSIVE:	Today I <u>am phoning</u>.
PAST PROGRESSIVE:	Yesterday I <u>was phoning</u>.
FUTURE PROGRESSIVE:	Tomorrow I <u>will be phoning</u>.
PRESENT PROGRESSIVE:	Today I <u>am hunting</u>.
PAST PROGRESSIVE:	Yesterday I <u>was hunting</u>.
FUTURE PROGRESSIVE:	Tomorrow I <u>will be hunting</u>.
PRESENT PROGRESSIVE:	Today I <u>am griping</u>.
PAST PROGRESSIVE:	Yesterday I <u>was griping</u>.
FUTURE PROGRESSIVE:	Tomorrow I <u>will be griping</u>.

In the **perfect progressive tenses**, we describe actions that have been in progress but were completed (or will be completed) in the present, past, or future.

The main verb is still an *-ing* form, and it always has two auxiliaries: a form of *have* followed by *been*. In fact, all the auxiliaries in all tenses of the perfect progressive are perfect tenses of the verb *be*. In the present perfect progress, the auxiliaries are *have been* or (with third-person singular subjects) *has been*. In the past, they are *had been*. And, of course, in the future perfect progressive, the auxiliaries are *will have been*.

PRESENT PERFECT PROGRESSIVE:	Today I <u>have been phoning</u>.
PAST PERFECT PROGRESSIVE:	Yesterday I <u>had been phoning</u>.
FUTURE PERFECT PROGRESSIVE:	By this time tomorrow I <u>will have been phoning</u>.
PRESENT PERFECT PROGRESSIVE:	Today I <u>have been hunting</u>.
PAST PERFECT PROGRESSIVE:	Yesterday I <u>had been hunting</u>.
FUTURE PERFECT PROGRESSIVE:	By this time tomorrow I <u>will have been hunting</u>.

PRESENT PERFECT PROGRESSIVE: Today I <u>have been grousing</u>.
PAST PERFECT PROGRESSIVE: Yesterday I <u>had been grousing</u>.
FUTURE PERFECT PROGRESSIVE: By this time tomorrow I <u>will have been grousing</u>.

THE THREE (OR FOUR) PRINCIPAL PARTS

Most English verbs have consistent verb forms that we use to create the tenses we've just examined. These are called **regular verbs**, which means that the form to create the past tense and the perfect tenses are the same. That is, in both the simple past tense and the perfect tenses, we add *–d* or *–ed*, or (in a few cases) add a final *-t*. No other change in spelling happens, as you'll see in the table below.

So we say that every verb (except some auxiliary verbs) has three **principal parts**: the present, the past, and the **past participle** (which is the form used with *have* for perfect tenses). These are usually presented in a table like this:

present	*past*	*past participle*
I talk	I talked	I have talked
I hunt	I hunted	I have hunted
I phone	I phoned	I have phoned
I build	I built	I have built

All of these are regular verbs. The past and past participle are the same word.

Notice the relatively new verb *to phone*. Newly-created English verbs are always regular: *fax, faxed; text, texted; friend, friended.* (But there is at least one exception: *We hung out at the mall.*)

When we speak of a *fourth* principal part, it's always the **present participle**, the *-ing* form used for progressive tenses: *talking, hunting, phoning, building.* And the *-ing* form is easy.

IRREGULAR VERBS

Irregular verbs are less consistent in their past and past participle forms. Although English has fewer irregular verbs than regular, there are hundreds of them. Many are among the most commonly used verbs in English.

Here are a small number:

present	*past*	*past participle*
I begin	I began	I have begun
I break	I broke	I have broken
I bring	I brought	I have brought
I drink	I drank	I have drunk
I drive	I drove	I have driven
I fly	I flew	I have flown
I freeze	I froze	I have frozen
I know	I knew	I have known
I ride	I rode	I have ridden
I ring	I rang	I have rung
I see	I saw	I have seen
I sink	I sank	I have sunk
I speak	I spoke	I have spoken
I swim	I swam	I have swum
I swing	I swung	I have swung
I take	I took	I have taken
I write	I wrote	I have written

All of us make errors now and then with some of the irregular verbs, and it's a good idea to identify those that give you the most trouble and study them. The table above gives you some of the most common irregulars, and you can find complete lists in many grammar books and on the Internet. A dictionary can always help you with specific verbs.

One way to study irregulars is to group the verbs that are similar in their past and past participle forms, like this:

present	*past*	*past participle*
I begin	I began	I have begun
I drink	I drank	I have drunk
I ring	I rang	I have rung
I sink	I sank	I have sunk
I swim	I swam	I have swum
I break	I broke	I have broken
I freeze	I froze	I have frozen
I speak	I spoke	I have spoken
I drive	I drove	I have driven
I ride	I rode	I have ridden
I write	I wrote	I have written
I fly	I flew	I have flown
I know	I knew	I have known

The following are verbs that you may also want to study. The verb *dive* is in fact regular:

| I dive | I dived | I have dived |

But *dove*, as a past and past participle, has become so common that it is now widely accepted.

We might call the verb *burst* "super-regular." It doesn't change at all:

Today I burst   Yesterday I burst   I have burst

Other super-regular verbs include *hit, set,* and *split.*

Shine is a peculiar case. Used as a **transitive verb** (which we'll study soon), it's regular*: They have shined their trophies every month.*

They shine   They shined   They have shined

As an **intransitive verb** (another term that's coming up), it's irregular: *The sun has shone all day.*

It shines   It shone   It had shone

The verb *hang* is also peculiar, taking different forms depending on its meaning. Imagine you're in a dusty little town in the Old West, and you ask a gnarled old-timer, "Whatever happened to that grammar teacher?" And the old-timer answers,

We've *hanged* that danged grammar teacher. He was all the time correctin' us!

But if you're proudly displaying your framed diploma on the wall, you could say,

I've finally *hung* my diploma.

There are six verbs (grouped in pairs below) that confuse us all at some point:

I <u>sit</u> down.   I <u>set</u> the books down.
I <u>lie</u> down.   I <u>lay</u> the books down.
I <u>rise</u> up.   I <u>raise</u> the books up.

In the left column, the verbs indicate the way you are positioning *yourself*. They are all irregular verbs. In the right column, the verbs indicate the way you are positioning the *object* (or anything else separate from yourself). They are all regular.

It's easy to keep these two sets of verbs straight: The verbs on the left all have the letter *i* as their first vowel. Remember that "the *i*-verbs indicate how *I* change my position."

Let's take a look at the principal parts of these three pairs of verbs. Notice that the second verb in each pair is regular. You probably know these already:

present	*past*	*past participle*
I sit	I sat	I have sat
I set	I set	I have set

You may also know these:

present	*past*	*past participle*
I rise	I rose	I have risen
I raise	I raised	I have raised

Perhaps the most difficult of all irregular verbs are *lie* and *lay*:

present	*past*	*past participle*
I lie (*recline*)	I lay	I have lain
I lay (*set down*)	I laid	I have laid
I lie (*fib*)	I lied	I have lied

As you see here, there are two verbs *to lie*. One means to *recline*, and one means *to fib*. *Lie* (*to fib*) is easy—it's a regular verb. *Lay* (*to set down*) is also a regular verb.

Lie (*to recline*) is irregular, and it confuses many people because its past form, *I lay*, is identical to the present form of *to lay* (*set down*).

To add to the confusion, in speech *I lay down* (the correct form) sounds exactly like *I laid down* (the wrong form), so we're often making mistakes because we're repeating the forms we hear—or think we hear. (The whole thing makes us want to lie down, no lie.)

It is probably accurate to say that many English speakers, perhaps most of us, misuse *lie* sometimes, but you can master it in a few moments and remember it with a little review now and then.

Even with irregular verbs, the past participle is always used with the auxiliary *have* (or its other forms *has* or *had*) to create perfect tenses (*have lain*). Forms of the verb *be* are always used with the *-ing* form (the present participle) to create progressive tenses.

EXERCISES

3a. Write from memory the simple and perfect tenses of the verb *call*.

3b. Write from memory the simple progressive and perfect progressive tenses of the verb *call*.

3c. Write from memory the simple and perfect tenses of the verb *know*.

3d. Write from memory the simple progressive and perfect progressive tenses of the verb *know*.

3e. Complete these sentences using the correct verb and the correct principal part:

    1. I will ____ here. (sit / set)

    2. I will ____ my suitcase in the corner. (sit / set)

3. I will ____ my bag to the top shelf. (rise / raise)

4. I will ____ from my seat. (rise / raise)

5. I have ____ from my seat. (risen / raised)

6. I have ____ my bag. (risen / raised)

7. I will ____ down. (lie / lay)

8. I will ____ my bag over here. (lie / lay)

9. I have ____ here for an hour. (lain / laid)

10. An hour ago, I ____ my bag there. (lain / laid)

3f. Complete the sentences using one or more auxiliary verbs:

1. The perfect tenses use forms of the auxiliary verb ____.

2. The progressive tenses use forms of the auxiliary verb ____.

3. The perfect progressive tenses use forms of two auxiliary verbs: ____ and ____.

4. All future tenses use the auxiliary ____.

3g. Identify the tense of the verb in each of the following sentences using one of these twelve terms:

- Simple past, present, or future
- Present perfect, past perfect, or future perfect
- Present progressive, past progressive, or future progressive

- Present perfect progressive, past perfect progressive, or future perfect progressive

1. She <u>was</u> here yesterday.

2. We <u>have been waiting</u> for you for an hour.

3. She <u>broke</u> her glasses.

4. She <u>has broken</u> her glasses twice.

5. Yesterday's news <u>burst</u> all our illusions.

6. I <u>will speak</u> to the principal.

7. I <u>will be speaking</u> to the principal.

8. We <u>had spoken</u> to the principal already.

9. You <u>will have been speaking</u> to the principal by now.

10. I <u>have sung</u> this song before.

3h. Complete the sentences using the names of principal parts of the verbs, or with the auxiliaries *will, have,* and *be.*

1. The perfect tenses are constructed using the third principal part, called the ____.

2. The progressive tenses are constructed using the fourth principal part, called the ____.

3. All future tense verbs begin with the auxiliary ____.

4. All perfect tenses are constructed using some form of the auxiliary ____.

5. All progressive tenses are constructed using some form of the auxiliary ____.

6. The tenses constructed using both the auxiliaries *have* and *be* are called the ____ tenses.

4 Tall, Dark, and Wordsome

Adjectives

MODIFIERS AND PHRASES

As we saw in Chapter 1, nouns and verbs often have modifiers, words that describe the noun or the verb.

The following examples are not sentences but only parts of sentences. Here *man* is the noun; all the other words before and after *man* are modifiers that restrict the meaning of *man* in some way:

<u>The</u> man
<u>The</u> man <u>in our neighborhood</u>
<u>The irritable, unfriendly</u> man <u>in our neighborhood</u>

As we've seen before, many modifiers appear immediately before the noun they modify: *The, irritable, unfriendly*. Some appear after: *in our neighborhood*.

This brings us to a common term that we use throughout these chapters: **phrase**. A phrase is a word or group of words used as a single grammatical unit.

The three examples above are **noun phrases**. They contain the noun *man* and other words and phrases that modify *man*.

Each of those noun phrases could be used as a single grammatical unit—for example, as the subject of a sentence. That is, the noun by itself would be the simple subject, and the noun and its modifiers would be the complete subject.

ADJECTIVES

Words like *irritable* and *unfriendly* are **adjectives**. Adjectives modify nouns and sometimes **pronouns**. They describe the noun or place limits on the word's range of reference. In the following noun phrases, all the underlined words are adjectives:

The <u>silvery</u> moon
The <u>light brown</u> hair
<u>Blue</u> skies

In most cases, adjectives simply describe nouns: *tall, short, ripe, rotten, round, perfect, clean, dirty, blank, full, empty, old, new, ancient, medieval, modern,* and thousands more.

THE THREE ARTICLES

There are only three **articles** in English: *a, an,* and *the*. Articles are always used to modify nouns. Some grammar books treat articles as if they are a separate class of words, but in this book we'll consider them a small, special subset of adjectives.

There is some confusion about when to use *a* and *an*. We use the article *a* before a word that begins with a consonant, and use *an* before a word that begins with a vowel, as in these phrases:

A child   An only child
A cheese omelet An omelet

But we're sometimes puzzled when we see *a* and *an* used in phrases like these:

<u>A union</u> of concerned citizens
<u>An honor</u> to work with you

So let's clarify the rules: Use *a* before a word beginning with a consonant sound (as in *a union* or *a child*):

A unicorn   An uninvited guest

Use *an* before a word beginning with a vowel sound (as in *an honor* or *an only child*):

A man   An honest man

The important consideration is the first sound (not the first letter) in the word following the article. This includes the first sound in abbreviations: *An M.D., a U. S. territory.*

Finally, *a* and *an* are called the **indefinite articles**. *The* is the only **definite article** in English, indicating a specific object that we can distinguish from all other objects of the same kind: *the last straw.*

ADJECTIVES AND WORD ORDER

In the noun phrases we've seen so far, the adjective appears before the noun. But adjectives can also appear immediately after the noun:

<u>The old</u> house, <u>dark</u> and <u>foreboding</u>
<u>The noisy</u> fairground, <u>bright</u> and <u>crowded</u>
<u>A glorious</u> sunset, <u>gold</u> and <u>lavender</u>

Articles are helpful in recognizing other adjectives. Consider this:

<u>The smaller</u> child learned <u>the simplest</u> tasks.

When a word appears between an article and a noun, it's an adjective or another word functioning as an adjective.

COMMON KINDS OF ADJECTIVES

There are certain groups of words that we can easily recognize as adjectives. Color words are often adjectives: *a blue moon, green apples*. (Sometimes, in a different context, color words are nouns: *a dark blue, a vivid red*.)

These color words are adjectives:

The <u>green</u> apples   The <u>gold and lavender</u> sunset
<u>Red</u> sails   <u>Red, white,</u> and <u>blue</u> bunting
A <u>blue</u> moon   A <u>yellow</u> traffic light

There are other descriptive words:

The <u>new</u> house   A <u>sentimental old</u> song
<u>Impulsive</u> behavior   <u>Exciting new</u> developments
A <u>generous</u> gift   <u>Soft</u> music

There are adjectives that indicate number or quantity:

<u>Both</u> friends   <u>One</u> sock
A <u>few</u> corrections   <u>Two</u> shirts
<u>Many</u> pages   <u>Three</u> shoes

Words that show possession are often used as adjectives:

<u>My</u> mistake   <u>Bob and Ray's</u> routine
<u>Your</u> complaint   <u>Wayne's</u> help
<u>His</u> insight   <u>Elizabeth's</u> reign

Some question words can be used as adjectives:

<u>Which</u> room?
<u>What</u> mess?
<u>Whose</u> responsibility?

We'll say it again: A good desk or online dictionary can help you identify adjectives and other words.

NOUNS AND VERBS USED ADJECTIVALLY

Sometimes we build a noun phrase by using nouns or verbs to modify a noun:

The <u>street</u> noise The <u>squeaking</u> wheel
The <u>traffic</u> accident A <u>frozen</u> lake

In these cases, we say that the noun or verb is used **adjectivally**, and we'll look at more cases of these in future chapters.

COMPARISONS OF ADJECTIVES

Some adjectives have three forms, which together make the **comparison** of the adjective:

Positive	*Comparative*	*Superlative*
hot	hotter	hottest
cold	colder	coldest
friendly	friendlier	friendliest
famous	more famous	most famous
suspicious	more suspicious	most suspicious
athletic	more athletic	most athletic

In any comparison of adjectives like these, there is a positive form of the adjective that simply names a quality the noun has: *hot, cold, friendly.*

We use the comparative when we're comparing two—and only two—items, and we use the superlative when we're comparing three or more:

Susan is a <u>fast</u> runner.
Susan is a <u>faster</u> runner than Alice.
In fact, she's the <u>fastest</u> runner of all.

As we see in these sentences, when we're comparing one-syllable adjectives (and some two-syllable adjectives), we create the comparative and superlative forms by adding the suffixes *–er* and *–est*. See the examples for *hot, cold,* and *friendly* in the table of comparisons above.

When we're comparing adjectives of three or more syllables (and some two-syllable adjectives), we create the comparative and superlative forms by placing the modifiers *more* and *most* before the adjectives. See the examples for *famous, suspicious,* and *athletic* in the table above.

When the comparison of an adjective is formed using the *-er* and *-est* suffices or the *more* and *most* adverbs, we refer to it as a **regular adjective**.

Some two-syllable adjectives, like those below, can take either kind of comparison:

happy, happier, happiest
happy, more happy, most happy.

often, oftener, oftenest
often, more often, most often

Many careful writers seem to prefer *happy, happier, happiest* and *often, more often, most often*. When in doubt about a comparison, turn to the dictionary. And *never* use both kinds of comparison with the same word:

WRONG: Ed is our <u>most hardest</u> working employee.

Some adjectives that describe absolute qualities cannot be compared logically: We don't usually say *deader* or *deadest*, or *more pregnant* or *most pregnant*, unless we're kidding around. And it usually doesn't make sense to say *more full* or *most instant* or *most continuous*.

But sometimes we ignore logic, especially in everyday conversation. *Unique* (meaning "one of a kind") is a well-known example. Logically, something is either unique or it isn't, but people will still say things like this:

That tire swing in their living room is a *very unique* feature.

They mean that it's an *unusual* feature. But in everyday conversation (as opposed to professional writing), it seldom matters if you say *very unique* or *most unique*.

Every now and then a careful writer will ignore all of these arguments and compare an absolute quality, and it works. The opening words of the Preamble of the United States Constitution are one such example:

We, the People of the United States, in Order to form a *more perfect* Union . . . .

No one we know of has ever objected.

POINTS FOR WRITERS

1. Know the irregular adjectives.

A few adjectives have comparisons that are like clothes you see marked down in the stores: They're **irregular adjectives**—they don't follow the usual patterns. They are some of the most commonly used adjectives, so you probably know most of them already:

Positive	Comparative	Superlative
bad	worse	worst
good	better	best
little	less	least
much (or *many*)	more	most

2. Use superlatives correctly.

Consider this sentence:

I've heard Barbra and Taylor sing. Barbra is the <u>best</u> singer.

By the strictest rules of usage, we should write *Barbra is the better singer*, because we're only comparing two singers. Using the superlative form in a comparison of two is common in casual conversation, but we should try to avoid it in careful writing unless we're deliberately developing an informal style.

3. Use hyphens in certain kinds of phrases.

When we use an entire phrase as an adjective, we typically hyphenate it:

> The four-year-old girl
> A by-the-numbers process
> The broken-down car
> The short-term solution

Some cases are a bit more complex. Consider this noun phrase:

> <u>Nineteenth-century</u> and <u>twentieth-century American</u> literature

We can remove one word and say the same thing:

> <u>Nineteenth-</u> and <u>twentieth-century American</u> literature

Notice the hanging hyphen after *nineteenth*. It enables *nineteenth* and *twentieth* to share the second element *century*. Here's another example:

> <u>Short-</u> and <u>long-term</u> solutions.

All the uses of hyphens shown here reflect formal usage. Increasingly, the hyphen is omitted in cases like these in less formal published prose.

EXERCISES

4a. Name the three articles.

4b. Identify the adjectives (including articles) in these sentences and underline them:

1. The new teacher is waiting in the outer office.

2. A rainy day could ruin the entire event.

3. Count Dracula is the tall, pale man in the shadows.

4. A backyard garden is a wonderful thing.

5. She wore a red and white dress to the casual party.

6. I gave my little brother good advice.

7. She has been a better student this year because of her hard work.

8. Bob's idea is the worst idea I've heard in a long time.

9. The point-by-point refutation was a difficult argument to follow.

10. Two roads lead to his farm.

11. Which roads are those?

4c. Give the comparative and superlative forms of these adjectives; use a dictionary when you need it. In some cases, there may be no comparative or superlative forms.

1. Small

2. Fast

3. Bright

4. Good

5. Bad

6. Curious

7. Cheerful

8. Happy

9. Wrong

10. Far (meaning anything except geographical distance)

5 Inevitably, Adverbs

Adverbs are another important kind of modifier. Here's a definition that we'll refer to time and again:

Adverbs are words that modify verbs, adjectives, and other adverbs.

When adverbs modify verbs, they indicate *when, where, why,* or *how* the action was performed.

Let's begin with the simple sentence *He ran. Ran* is a verb and the complete predicate in this sentence, and we can expand the predicate by adding any possible adverb:

He ran <u>quickly</u>.

Instead of *quickly*, we could use *slowly, clumsily, gracefully, erratically, fast, then, later,* and many others.

All the adverbs we can add to *He ran* answer this question: "When, where, why, or how did he run?" Common adverbs that modify verbs include *soon, later, now, then, before, after, here, there, forward, backward, badly, well, far, also, not, too,* and many more.

Remember the point we saw in Chapter 3: When a word appears between an auxiliary verb and the main verb, it's an adverb that modifies the main verb:

He had <u>finally</u> stopped the noise.

Remember, too, that all the adverbs we add to a sentence to modify the verb are part of the complete predicate.

When adverbs modify adjectives, they appear before the adjective and modify the quality expressed by the adjective:

The <u>bright</u> red car sped away.

We use (and overuse) several adverbs to modify adverbs, particularly *very*. We could write *quite, extremely, somewhat,* or *rather*. Here, the adverb helps to describe the color of the red car.

When adverbs modify other adverbs, adverbs modify the quality expressed by the other adverb:

Mr. Morton ran <u>quite</u> quickly.

Instead of *quite*, we could write *somewhat, very, a bit, rather, more,* or *less*. Here, adverbs answer the question, "How quickly did Mr. Morton run?"

Notice that, when adverbs modify adjectives or other adverbs, they nearly always appear just before the word they modify.

Clearly adverbs are a diverse class of words; they have a great many uses and forms.

COMPARISONS OF ADVERBS

Some adverbs, like many adjectives, have three forms, which together make the **comparison** of the adverb:

Positive	Comparative	Superlative
close	closer	closest
fast	faster	fastest
early	earlier	earliest
warmly	more warmly	most warmly
generously	more generously	most generously
suspiciously	more suspiciously	most suspiciously

Here again, we use the positive when we're describing the action or quality of one thing, we use the comparative when we're comparing two (and only two), and we use the superlative when we're comparing three or more.

A relatively small number of adverbs form comparisons with the *-er* and *-est* suffixes:

Susan runs <u>fast</u>.
Susan runs <u>faster</u> than Alice.
In fact, she runs <u>fastest</u> of all.

The examples above show that some adverbs (like *fast*) resemble adjectives with little or no difference in spelling or pronunciation, but with a clear difference in their use. This is obvious if we compare the three sentences above about Susan with the similar sentences we saw in Chapter 4:

Susan is a <u>fast</u> runner.
Susan is a <u>faster</u> runner than Alice.
In fact, she's the <u>fastest</u> runner of all.

With *fast* (and some words like it), we can distinguish the adverb *fast* from the adjective *fast* only by the context. When we use a word like *fast* to modify a verb, grammarians say that we use it *adverbially*.

Most of the adverbs that end with *-ly* use the *more* and *most* comparisons. Dictionaries can always help you find the right forms.

THOSE MOST IRREGULAR COMPARISONS

There are also irregular adverbs that don't follow the usual patterns. They are some of the most commonly used adverbs, so you know most of them already:

Positive	*Comparative*	*Superlative*
badly	worse	worst
well	better	best
little	less	least
much (or *many*)	more	most
far	farther	farthest
	further	furthest

Far requires some attention. In prescriptive grammar, *far, farther,* and *farthest* are supposed to be used to describe physical distance:

He ran <u>farther</u> than I did.

Far, further, and *furthest* are to be used in every other kind of situation:

He went <u>further</u> in school than I did.

It's no surprise that some writers find this distinction unnecessary, especially because most Americans aren't even aware of it. These writers argue that the adverb is always clear no matter which form is used, so we need to settle on one set of comparisons and use it in most or all situations.

But there is no clear consensus on how to simplify the *far* comparison. (That word is *far* too troublesome.) In your professional writing, an editor or supervisor may expect you to do it the prescriptive way.

NOUNS USED ADVERBIALLY

Used correctly, other words can modify verbs—particularly nouns that specify *where, how,* or *when* the action occurred:

We walked home.
We walked single file.

This may seem odd, but it will be clearer when we discuss form, function, and parts of speech in Chapter 16.

Nouns regarding time are commonly used **adverbially**:

They celebrated her birthday yesterday.
Tomorrow we go on vacation.
Monday we return from vacation.
They worked in the yard Saturday.

Nouns can also function adverbially to modify adjectives. In these sentences, the modified adjective is in bold:

My son is now four feet tall.
My daughter is two inches taller.
They worked all day long.

Finally, adverbial nouns can modify other adverbs. In these sentences, the modified adverbs are in bold:

I wish we had left a day later.
We can go ten miles farther.

CURIOUS ADVERBS: WHEN, WHERE, WHY, AND HOW

When, where, why, and *how* are four of the most important adverbs in our language. They are the **interrogative adverbs**, the ones we use to ask questions. We usually place them at or near the beginning of a question:

Where are you going?
When will you be back?

There are of course other useful question words, like *who* or *what*, but those are **interrogative pronouns**, which we'll learn about in Chapter 19.

In this chapter, we've learned that nouns can be used adverbially, and the interrogative adverbs return the favor. Sometimes they are used as nouns:

I know I'm supposed to be someplace today, but I can't remember where or when.

POINTS FOR WRITERS

1. Place adverbs correctly.

Adverbs that modify verbs are often moveable; they can be placed in several places in the sentence without changing the meaning:

Quickly Phil called the police.
Phil quickly called the police.
Phil called the police quickly.

Quietly the children hurried home.
The children quietly hurried home.
The children hurried home quietly.

Then he ran.
He then ran.
He ran then.

The three underlined adverbs obviously work in several places in the sentence. Moving them doesn't alter the meaning, although it may alter the rhythm or emphasis in the sentence. But moving some words, like *only* or *however*, can change the meaning:

Only Mr. Morton broke the vase.
  [Mr. Morton broke it all by himself.]

Mr. Morton only broke the vase.
  [He didn't do anything else to it.]

Mr. Morton broke only the vase.
  [He didn't break anything else—yet.]

As we move *only*, the new contexts change its meaning in the sentences above. (In the first sentence, *only* is an adjective.)

2. Distinguish good and well.

Writing for publication or for other professional reasons, you must observe the distinction between *good* and *well*:

He is a good writer.
He writes well. [Never write *He writes good*.]

Good is an adjective. *Well* is sometimes an adverb and sometimes an adjective, depending on context. It can be an adjective meaning *healthy*, in sentences like this:

Finally my son is well.

It's hard to use *well* well. Probably everyone has confused *good* and *well* in casual conversation at one time or another, and there it seldom matters. But readers and editors will assume that you're a careless writer if you confuse the two in your professional work.

EXERCISES

These exercises refer to matters you've read about in the last two chapters. Don't hesitate to turn back to Chapter 4 if you need to review.

5a. In the following sentences, mark the underlined words to classify them as adjectives (*ADJ*) or adverbs (*ADV*). Count the articles *a, an,* and *the* as adjectives. The adverbs here modify verbs only. Here are examples to help:

ADJ ADJ
This is <u>a pleasant</u> day.

ADJ ADJ   ADV
<u>The small</u> child runs <u>quickly.</u>

ADJ ADJ   ADV
<u>The other</u> child runs <u>faster</u>.

1. <u>The smaller</u> child learned <u>the simplest</u> tasks.

2. <u>The</u> child learns <u>eagerly</u>.

3. John <u>almost</u> had <u>an</u> answer to <u>the difficult</u> question.

4. Father <u>always</u> encourages <u>realistic</u> thinking.

5. <u>The furious</u> family did <u>not</u> wait to see <u>the busy</u> manager.

6. <u>A thick, wet</u> snow fell <u>softly</u>.

7. <u>Silently</u>, <u>a strange</u> man in <u>a black</u> cape stood in <u>the</u> shadows.

5b. Write the comparative and superlative forms of these adverbs; use a dictionary when you need to.

1. Fast

2. Quickly

3. Slowly

4. Angrily

5. Carefully

6. Well

7. Badly

8. Early

9. Far (referring to geographical distance)

10. Often

5c. In these sentences, classify the underlined adverbs: Do they modify verbs, adjectives, or other adverbs?

1. Your mistake was a <u>very</u> small one.

2. He does <u>well</u> when he tries <u>hard</u>.

3. He does <u>quite</u> well when he tries.

4. The secretary's notes are <u>evidently</u> missing.

5. <u>Now</u> we <u>finally</u> have the notes.

6. We took notes <u>rather</u> <u>rapidly</u>, but we could <u>not</u> keep up.

7. We <u>still</u> need good notes.

5d. Correct the errors in the underlined adjectives and adverbs, which may include suffixes or, in some cases, the placement of the word. Some are correct.

1. Esther and Ryan play <u>good</u>, but Esther plays <u>best</u>.

2. By sunset we will have hiked ten miles or <u>further</u>.

3. The library has the <u>most complete book</u> on baseball.

4. Bob was the student <u>only</u> left behind. [Here the writer is trying to say that no one else was left behind.]

5. <u>Final</u> we reached the motel.

6. Be <u>real</u> careful on this highway.

7. We saw that Bart looked <u>sadly</u>.

8. Bart was looking <u>sad</u> at his wrecked car.

9. Bart was feeling <u>sadly</u> on his way home.

10. In the lab, we measured the results as <u>precise</u> as we could.

6 Among the Prepositions

Prepositions are short, simple, and remarkably useful words. We use prepositions to create modifying phrases called **prepositional phrases**.

With **prepositions** we can connect a noun phrase—called the **object of the preposition**—to another word in a sentence. The preposition and its object together make the prepositional phrase. A prepositional phrase usually modifies a noun or verb, but it can also modify an adjective or adverb.

Here are some examples of prepositional phrases. The prepositions are underlined, and the remaining words are the objects of the prepositions (with modifiers, in some cases):

<u>among</u> the debris   <u>beside</u> our house
<u>on</u> the roof   <u>from</u> the roof
<u>in</u> the room   <u>by</u> the room
<u>to</u> our house   <u>after</u> dinner
<u>for</u> your birthday   <u>with</u> her

As you see, prepositions usually *precede* their objects—that is, they are *pre-positioned* before the objects.

In English, there are hundreds of thousands of nouns, verbs, adjectives, and adverbs, but there are relatively few prepositions—

perhaps one hundred or so. The list below contains most of the frequently used prepositions.

If you read over the following list (about seventy) now and then, and refer to it when you need to, it will be easier for you to recognize prepositional phrases. And dictionaries can always help you recognize them:

aboard	besides	past
about	between	save
above	beyond	than
across	but (meaning *except*)	since
after	by	through
against	despite	throughout
along	down	till
alongside	during	to
amid	except	toward
amidst	for	towards
among	from	under
amongst	in	underneath
around	into	unlike
as	like	until
astride	near	up
at	of	upon
atop	off	with
before	on	within
behind	onto	without
below	out	worth
beneath	outside	
beside	over	

We'll look at more prepositions shortly.

The most important characteristic of a preposition is that it's usually followed by its object. You have to be careful about classifying a word as a preposition, because many of them act as other kinds of words—especially as adverbs. Some can also be special kinds of words that we'll study later, such as **participles** or as **particles** in **phrasal verbs**. A dictionary can help you make the distinction.

MORE EXAMPLES

Prepositional phrases serve a remarkable variety of purposes. Here are a few of their common uses, with prepositional phrases in the right-hand columns in the examples below.

Prepositional phrases often indicate *relative spatial positions*, as in these examples modifying nouns (i.e., they're all adjectival phrases):

the alley	behind [or beside] our house, on our block
the shingles	on top of our house
the shingle	on the roof
the plate	in the cupboard, by itself
the shoe	under [or by] the sofa, without the other
the picture	above the sofa, of Dorian Gray

Prepositional phrases often indicate *relative direction of movement*, as in these adverbial examples:

driving	by your house, down the street
going	to your house, up the street
going	into [or in] your house
going	through [or around] your house
leaving	from your house
throwing	at your house

(Well, *that* relationship went downhill in a hurry.)

Prepositional phrases can also indicate *time relationships*, as in these adverbial examples:

We'll meet   <u>after</u> the film.
We'll meet   <u>at</u> 8 pm.
We'll meet   <u>during</u> the meeting.
We'll meet   <u>before</u> dinner.
We'll meet   <u>for</u> twenty minutes.
We'll meet   <u>until</u> 8 pm.

And some prepositional phrases are just *creepy*:

The old house   <u>at</u> the top <u>of</u> the hill
The motel   <u>in</u> the middle <u>of</u> nowhere
The woman   <u>in</u> the shower

ADJECTIVAL OR ADVERBIAL?

As we've just seen, prepositional phrases are used as adjectives or adverbs—that is, they're used adjectivally or adverbially. Adjectival prepositional phrases usually follow the nouns they modify. The following sentences contain adjectival prepositional phrases, and we've underlined the entire phrase:

The dog <u>in the yard</u> barked loudly.
I read the first <u>of three volumes</u>.
This is my letter <u>to the principal</u>.

In each of the sentences above, the prepositional phrase modifies the noun it follows.

In the sentences below, the adverbial prepositional phrases are underlined:

    I arrived <u>at noon</u>.
    I drove <u>into the garage</u>.
    I walked <u>for exercise</u>.
    I walked <u>at a fast pace</u>.

As adverbs, these prepositional phrases tell us *when, where, why, or how* the action of the verb was performed.

We learned earlier that adverbs modifying verbs are often movable. In the sentences below, we see that some of the underlined adverbial prepositional phrases are also movable. Typically, the moveable phrases indicate *time, place, or manner*:

The dog barked loudly <u>in the yard</u>.
<u>In the yard</u>, the dog barked loudly.

Little Ruthie practiced the violin <u>for two hours</u>.
<u>For two hours</u>, little Ruthie practiced the violin.

Mr. Lochenhocher would rather listen <u>to the dog</u>.

I've heard Ruthie play, and I'm <u>with Lochenhocher</u>.

We can't move the adverbial prepositional phrases in the last two sentences.

Sometimes the guidelines for distinguishing adverbial and adjectival phrases don't work as well as we'd like. Here's another example:

We drove the car <u>into the garage</u>.

<u>Into the garage</u> follows *car*, but the phrase obviously doesn't modify *car*. Here the prepositional phrase is adverbial; it answers the question, "Where did you drive the car?" But this adverbial phrase is *not* moveable. We probably wouldn't write

<u>Into the garage</u>, we drove the car.

When we're trying to identify the function of the prepositional phrase, the most important point to consider is the meaning of the phrase. Does it reasonably apply to a noun or an action? What does it describe?

In other words, sometimes prepositional phrases—and other structures—are grammatically ambiguous. Consider this:

Steve read the book <u>in the living room</u>.

Does *in the living room* describe the book Steve read? That is, he read the book that was *in the living room*. In that case, the phrase is adjectival.

But it might be adverbial: Steve was *in the living room* when he read the book. The sentence can plausibly be read either way, which is not at all unusual.

To clarify, we could rewrite it this way:

<u>In the living room</u>, Steve read the book.

Now the phrase is unmistakably adverbial.

There's more. Adverbial prepositional phrases can also modify adjectives and adverbs. Below, they modify the adjectives *sure* and *careless*:

He was too **sure** <u>of himself</u>.

He was **careless** <u>with the dynamite</u>.

(By the way, both of the adjectives above are called **predicate adjectives**, which we'll learn about later.)

Next, these prepositional phrases modify the adverb *far*:

Musial hit the ball **far** <u>into left field</u>.

We steered the boat **far** <u>from the dock</u>.

In the four examples above, the prepositional phrases follow the words they modify. These adverbial uses are less common than those modifying verbs, and they are not moveable.

CONCERNING AND REGARDING OTHERS

Along with those we've seen so far, there are more one-word prepositions that are unusual, because they look like verbs. Specifically, they're the *–ing* form of verbs. Here's a list of common ones, with objects:

barring bad weather	*including* her
concerning the budget	*pending* your letter
considering the circumstances	*respecting* your question
counting you	*regarding* that issue
excepting me	*saving* one last preposition
following the instructions	*touching* the matter

Some of these look like **participles** (which are *–ing* verbs used adjectivally, a category we examine in Chapter 17). They may have begun life that way. (Words sometimes go downhill like that.)

Even the first list of prepositions contained one *–ing* word: *during*, with is a form of a verb we no longer use: *dure*, meaning *endure*.

Other prepositions that look a bit like participles include *given* and *notwithstanding:*

Given the weather, we should cancel the trip.
Notwithstanding the weather, we'll go anyway.

Some authorities don't accept all of the words above as prepositions.

PHRASAL PREPOSITIONS

This kind of preposition consists of a two-word phrase used as if it were one word. In the following examples, these phrasal prepositions are underlined:

<u>according to</u> the Bible
<u>as for</u> Steve
<u>because of</u> the time
<u>depending on</u> the weather
<u>except for</u> Patrick

<u>instead of</u> Stephanie
<u>out of</u> flour
<u>owing to</u> the weather
<u>up to</u> you

But grammatical categories can be porous, and sometimes authorities disagree about a word or phrase. Some grammar books and dictionaries identify the following phrases (or others like them) as prepositions:

<u>ahead of</u> you
<u>alongside of</u> you
<u>apart from</u> you
<u>away from</u> you
<u>close to</u> you

<u>contrary to</u> opinion
<u>due to</u> him
<u>next to</u> you
<u>together with</u> you

But there's another way to analyze phrases like these. The first word could be read as an adjective or adverb depending on context, followed by a one-word preposition and its object (*of you, from you,* and the others).

For example, the prepositional phrases in the following sentences are *adverbial*, modifying the adjectives and adverbs they follow:

We are ahead <u>of them</u>.
We are next <u>to them</u>.
Events were contrary <u>to expectations</u>.
We pulled alongside <u>of the truck</u>.

Some authorities classify the following three-word phrases (and a few others) as prepositions:

 by means of in back of in case of
 in charge of in front of in search of

But in their usual contexts, these are better analyzed as a series of *two* prepositional phrases, as in these examples:

 By <u>means</u>   **of** <u>law</u>, the project will be stopped.
 He is **in** <u>charge</u> **of** <u>the unit</u>.
 She is **in** <u>front</u>   **of** <u>the audience</u>.
 Call me **in** <u>case</u>   **of** <u>an emergency</u>.

So we'll claim that prepositions are never more than two words long. But don't be surprised if you encounter grammar books and dictionaries that recognize some three-word English phrases as "phrasal prepositions" or "compound prepositions."

LA PRÉPOSITION

One remaining sub-class of prepositions are words borrowed from Latin and French. You'll encounter them seldom, but most have their uses in certain contexts.

 à la [meaning "in the manner of"]
 He attempted to write <u>à la H. P. Lovecraft</u>.

 bar [meaning "except for"]
 She is the best, <u>bar none</u>.

 circa [meaning "in approximately"]
 Chaucer was born <u>circa 1340</u>.

cum [meaning "together with"]
He has built an office <u>cum workshop</u>.

per [meaning "for every"]
This car gets twenty-one miles <u>per gallon</u>.

re [meaning "about"]
We are writing <u>re your complaint</u>.

versus [meaning "against"; abbreviated *v.*]
We studied the famous case of *Griswold v. Connecticut*.

via [meaning "by way of"]
We traveled <u>via the Interminable Turnpike</u>.

vis-à-vis [meaning "compared with"]
We will consider our expenses <u>vis-à-vis our income</u>.

In general, avoid these prepositions unless the context justifies them. Using them carelessly makes you seem pretentious, and there are perfectly good English words and phrases that you can use instead.

POINTS FOR WRITERS

1. Should you end a sentence with a preposition?

One of the best-known rules of prescriptive grammar insists that we must never end sentences with prepositions. But, in fact, good professional writers do it all the time.

You should be aware, however, that in formal contexts, some writers and editors regard sentences like the following as too informal or just plain wrong:

He is the person <u>who</u> I want you to give this <u>to</u>.

This sentence troubles some readers for one or two reasons. First, the preposition *to* is no longer before its object, *who*. In fact, the preposition and its object are widely separated. Second, by the strictest rules of grammar, *who* should be *whom*.

Some editors and writers would prefer this version of the sentence:

He is the person <u>to whom</u> I want you to give this.

Still other editors might find this corrected version excessively formal for some purposes and readers because of *whom* and the placement of the prepositional phrase.

If necessary, we can usually rewrite an entire sentence to eliminate problems like these, as the next two possible revisions show:

Give this to him.
He should get this.

2. Unnecessary prepositions.

It's always a mistake to add an unnecessary preposition to a sentence. Here are some examples:

She got off <u>of</u> the train this morning.
Where did you find her <u>at</u>?
She was waiting beside <u>of</u> the station.

These are not colossal errors, but deleting unnecessary words is always a good thing to do.

EXERCISES

6a. In the following sentences <u>underline</u> the prepositional phrases and <u>double-underline</u> the preposition. Some sentences contain more than one prepositional phrase. If you need to, refer to the lists of prepositions in this chapter.

1. In the morning, I drink coffee with cream.

2. As a rule, I never put sugar in it.

3. Amid cars and trucks, Edwina ran across the street.

4. I am looking for the owner of this dog.

5. Are you referring to the dog that is nipping at your leg?

6. Throughout the book, the author emphasizes the influence of history upon our perception of events.

7. Like Arthur, I walked down the hall and paid no attention to the noise within the office.

8. According to Arthur, the noise out of the office was because of an argument between Ed and Grace.

9. Arthur should not have been left in charge of the office during the summer.

10. In case of further conflicts, we should make plans regarding appropriate training for all employees.

6b. After you finish Exercise 6a, go back through the ten sentences above and decide if the prepositional phrases are adjectival (ADJ) or adverbial (ADV), and label them accordingly.

Remember that adjectival prepositional phrases usually follow the nouns they modify and describe those nouns in some way.

Adverbial prepositional phrases often follow the verb or appear at the beginning of the sentence. Adverbials tell us *when, where, why, or how* the action takes place. They are often moveable.

7 You and I and the Personal Pronouns

Have *we* got a chapter for *you*. We've seen that nouns can be the simple subjects in sentences. There is another kind of word that can be a simple subject (and can play other roles in a sentence). It's the **pronoun**: a word that takes the place of a noun that appeared earlier in the context.

Common English pronouns include *I, me, mine, you, yours, he, she, it, him, her, his, hers,* and others.

When a pronoun takes the place of a noun, the noun replaced is called the **antecedent** of the pronoun. The antecedent usually appears before (*ante-*) its pronoun.

In the sentences that follow, the pronouns are underlined. Not all of them are subjects:

Gershwin composed.
He composed.
    (*Gershwin* is the antecedent of *He*.)

George loves Ethel.
He loves her.
    (*George* is the antecedent of *He*, and *Ethel* is the antecedent of *her*.)

Pearl painted Mr. Morton's porch.
<u>She</u> painted <u>his</u> porch.
>(*Pearl* is the antecedent of *She*, and *Mr. Morton* is the antecedent of *his*.)

<u>She</u> enjoyed painting <u>it</u>.
>(*Porch* is the antecedent of *it*.)

THE PERSONAL PRONOUNS

There are thousands of nouns in English but only a few dozen pronouns, and those we use most are called the **personal pronouns**. All of the pronouns in the sentences above, and all that we discuss in this chapter, are personal pronouns.

The following tables contain all of the personal pronouns in English, organized according to their several characteristics:

Singular Personal Pronouns

	Nominative	*Objective*	*Possessive*
First Person	I	me	my, mine
Second Person	you	you	your, yours
Third Person	he, she, it	him, her, it	his, her, hers, its

Notice that the third-person singular pronouns also have gender: *he, she,* or *it*.

Plural Personal Pronouns

	Nominative	*Objective*	*Possessive*
First Person	we	us	our, ours
Second Person	you	you	your, yours
Third Person	they	them	their, theirs

Notice that the possessive pronouns like *yours, hers,* and *theirs* don't contain apostrophes. The tables also show us that all personal pronouns are classified by number, singular or plural.

PRONOUNS AND PERSON

All personal pronouns are also classified by **person**. If you're referring to *yourself* with pronouns, you use first-person pronouns: *I, me, my*, and *mine*, or the plural forms *we, us, our*(s).

If you're referring to the person you're speaking with, you use second-person pronouns: *you* and *your*(s). The plural forms are the same.

If you're referring to another person outside the conversation, you use third-person pronouns:

he, she, it;
him, her, it; and
his, her, its (or the plurals *they, them, their,* and *theirs*)

The third-person singular pronouns are also classified by **gender**: masculine (*he, him, his*), feminine (*she, her, hers*), and neuter (*it, its*).

PRONOUNS AND CASE

Finally, we classify personal pronouns by cases: the **nominative case**, the **possessive case**, and the **objective case**. These terms are used all the time in discussions of language, so it's helpful to understand them. They refer to the forms of the pronouns that we use in certain positions in a sentence.

The pronouns in the **nominative case** are the ones we use as subjects:

I talked to Mr. Morton.
You talked to Mr. Morton.

<u>He</u> talked to Mr. Morton.
<u>She</u> talked to Mr. Morton.
<u>We</u> talked to Mr. Morton.
<u>They</u> talked to Mr. Morton, too, but <u>he</u> is still juggling vases.

The pronouns in the **possessive case** are used to indicate possession, and most of the possessive pronouns have two forms:

Hey, that's <u>my</u> vase.   (Or, That vase is <u>mine</u>.)
Hey, that's <u>your</u> vase.   (Or, That vase is <u>yours</u>.)
Hey, that's <u>his</u> vase.   (That vase is <u>his</u>.)
Hey, that's <u>her</u> vase.   (Or, That vase is <u>hers</u>.)
Hey, that's <u>our</u> vase.   (Or, That vase is <u>ours</u>.)
Hey, that's <u>their</u> vase.   (Or, That vase is <u>theirs</u>.)

Notice that there are no apostrophes in these –*s* possessives, or in *its*. This frequently confuses inexperienced writers. Apostrophes show possession only with nouns: *yours, ours, theirs,* but *children's, women's, Ruthie's, Pearl's, Mr. Morton's.*

The pronouns in the **objective case** are used for almost every other purpose in a sentence. For example, when pronouns are the objects of prepositions, they are always in the objective case:

I gave the book <u>to Julie</u>. I gave it <u>to her</u>.
Mike said that I can ride <u>with him</u>.
Give the vase to <u>me</u>.
Give it to <u>us</u>.
Give it to <u>them</u>.

If we're native speakers of English, we typically use the correct cases naturally. What we may have trouble remembering, as students of grammar, are terms for the three cases and the forms they describe. If you need to, you can learn this simple test sentence to help you remember the terms for the three cases of pronouns:

<u>N</u> took <u>O</u> to <u>P's</u> house.

Here, obviously, *N, O,* and *P* stand for the three cases: *nominative, objective,* and *possessive.* Insert the right pronoun in each position, and you will know the case of the pronouns in question:

<u>He</u> took <u>her</u> to <u>their</u> house.
<u>They</u> took <u>us</u> to <u>her</u> house.
<u>We</u> took <u>them</u> to <u>his</u> house.

In each case, the first pronoun is nominative, the second objective, and the third possessive.

The personal pronouns are the most important pronouns in English. We'll examine other kinds later.

BE TENSE!

Because we're learning about the matter of person in this chapter, it seems like a good time to return to verbs briefly, and to one in particular.

The verb *to be* is the most frequently used verb in English, and it's also the most irregular verb. Because its irregular forms are tied up with the matter of person, we'll examine *be* in detail here.

These are the simple tenses of *be*. Notice how the forms change in the first, second, and third person, as well as in the singular and plural:

Singular	*Present*	*Past*	*Future*
1st person	I am	I was	I will be
2nd person	You are	You were	You will be
3rd person	He is	He was	He will be

Plural	Present	Past	Future
1st person	We are	We were	We will be
2nd person	You are	You were	You will be
3rd person	They are	They were	They will be

Notice that the second-person forms are identical in the singular and plural. Notice, too, that there is great variety in the singular tenses, which use six different forms (*am, are, is, was, were,* and *be*), but the plurals are more consistent.

As we move from the simple tenses to the tenses that require more auxiliaries, there is less variation in *be*. For that reason, we'll look only at the singular in the following tenses.

These are the perfect tenses of *be*:

Singular	Present	Past	Future
1st person	I have been	I had been	I will have been
2nd person	You have been	You had been	You will have been
3rd person	She has been	he had been	She will have been

In the perfect tense, the main verb is always the past participle, *been*, and the auxiliaries *have, had,* and *has* show tense and number in every tense but the future.

These are the progressive tenses of *be*:

Singular	Present	Past	Future
1st person	I am being	I was being	I will be being
2nd person	You are being	You were being	You will be being
3rd person	He is being	He was being	He will be being

Notice here and in the perfect progressive tense (which is below) that the main verb is always *being*. But the first auxiliary verb in these tenses show considerable variation: *am, are, is, was,* and *were*.

These are the perfect progressive tenses of *be*:

Singular	Present	Past	Future
1st person	I have been being	I had been being	I will have been being
2nd person	You have been being	You had been being	You will have been being
3rd person	He has been being	He had been being	He will have been being

POINTS FOR WRITERS

1. Use objective case pronouns as objects of prepositions.

Sometimes you see nominative case pronouns used as objects of the prepositions:

WRONG: Between Bob and I, we'll get the job done.
WRONG: Give the responsibility to Susan and I.

But the nominative case is never right in this position. Always use the objective case as the object of the preposition:

Between Bob and me, we'll get the job done.
Give the report to Susan and me.

In the second example, you can make certain that you have the right pronoun by leaving out Susan: Give *the report to me*. If *me* is right in that sentence, it's also right when used in *to Susan and me*.

In both sentences, plural pronouns like *us* could also work in place of the two objects, but the pronouns must still be in the objective case.

By the way, there is no grammatical reason to put *me* last in the two examples above; it's a matter of courtesy. And courtesy is important, too.

2. Use pronoun gender carefully.

The third-person singular pronouns (*he, she, it,* and the others) can be troublesome. Consider this passage:

> Each physician should submit <u>his</u> credentials to the hospital's human resources department. Each nurse must submit <u>her</u> credentials, too.

In the past, these sentences may have been completely acceptable to most readers and editors. As you know, they are *not* acceptable today. Most readers and editors object to the apparent assumption that all physicians are men and all nurses are women.

Today the usual way to avoid this problem, and the way we recommend in most cases, is to make the sentence plural:

> <u>All physicians and nurses</u> must submit <u>their</u> credentials to the hospital's human resources department.

Sometimes we can omit pronouns altogether:

> All physicians and nurses must submit credentials . . . .

Other ways, like the use of *his or her* or *his/her*, are possible, but some editors regard them as awkward or wordy.

There's still another way. Today *they, them,* and *their* are sometimes used as singular pronouns, when you don't know the gender of the antecedent:

Tell your doctor to send me their diagnosis of your case.

Some people approve, and some don't, so (in certain professional contexts) tread carefully *and consider the context*. Again, you can rewrite the sentence to sidestep the entire issue: *Send me the diagnosis* . . . .

3. Avoid pronoun ambiguity.

Used carelessly, pronouns can be confusing.

> CONFUSING: The speaker discussed the causes of the recession, but I didn't understand it at all.

> BETTER: In his speech, the speaker discussed the causes of the recession, but I didn't understand him at all.

> BETTER: The speaker discussed the causes of the recession in his speech, but I didn't understand it at all.

These three sentences demonstrate the importance of selecting the right pronouns for your context. This is called **pronoun agreement**. When writers neglect pronoun agreement, they often confuse their readers.

Here are two more examples of pronoun ambiguity. In these sentences, what is the antecedent of *she*?

> Sally's mother has collected dolls since she was twelve years old.

> Sally told her mother that she was too old to play with dolls.

The reader shouldn't have to guess who *she* is. It's usually easy to rewrite the sentences to avoid ambiguity:

Sally's mother has collected dolls for twenty-three years.

Sally thought that her mother was too old to play with dolls and told her so.

(Sally is asking for trouble.)

4. Maintain a consistent point of view.

That is, don't change pronouns unnecessarily. Consider the confused point of view in this paragraph:

When <u>you</u> have worked with adolescents for a few months, <u>you</u> will know what to expect. People who work with adolescents learn quickly what problems <u>they</u> will encounter in most situations. <u>You</u> get to know how <u>they</u> think.

Don't shift point of view without a good reason. Be consistent in your use of pronouns. Use third person or, when reasonable, first person, or a careful combination of first and third.

Use second person (*you*) when it makes sense to address the reader directly.

Here's an improved version of the same paragraph:

After <u>you</u> have worked with adolescents for a few months, <u>you</u> will know what to expect. <u>You</u> will quickly learn what problems <u>you</u> will encounter in most situations. <u>You</u> will get to know how <u>they</u> think.

Inexperienced writers sometimes overuse the second-person pronouns, but it is usually acceptable in instructions like the passage above, or in personal communications like letters and emails. The second-person is also useful in establishing a more informal, conversational tone, as we have done in these chapters.

It is also grammatical to use the indefinite pronoun *one* in passages like this:

> After <u>one</u> has worked with adolescents for a few months, <u>one</u> will know what to expect. <u>One</u> quickly learns what problems will be encountered in most situations.

This use of *one* is now often seen as excessively formal and impersonal, and even awkward. Using *you* is usually a better idea.

5. Use pronouns precisely.

Using *they, you,* and *it* imprecisely is often a symptom of careless writing:

> WRONG: <u>They</u> don't allow <u>you</u> to build fires in the city park.

> BETTER: <u>The city</u> doesn't allow <u>anyone</u> to build fires in the city park.

> WRONG: <u>It</u> says in the letter that your band, Noise Pollution, is banned from performing in the city limits.

> BETTER: <u>The City Council</u> says in its letter that your band, Noise Pollution, is banned from performing in the city limits.

EXERCISES

7a. In this exercise, you need to write five versions of the same short sentence. Each version will use a different pronoun.

First read the pronouns in the parentheses after each sentence. Then, for each pronoun, find the correct case to insert into the blank. Consult the pronoun tables in this chapter if you need to.

Example:

> Give the book to _____. (I, he, we, they, she)

> Give the book to <u>me</u>.
> Give the book to <u>him.</u>
> Give the book to <u>us</u>.
> Give the book to <u>them.</u>
> Give the book to <u>her</u>.

As you can see, to complete the sentence, you needed the **objective** case for each of the requested pronouns (*I, he, we, they, she*).

Use the **objective** case in these sentences:

> 1. You can go with _____. (I, he, we, they, she)
> 2. We will take _____ to the mall. (he, she, they, you)

Use the **nominative** case in this sentence:

> 3. _____ can go with me. (him, her, you, them, us)

Use the **possessive** case in these sentences:

> 4. That book isn't yours. It's _____. (I, he, we, they, she)
> 5. We won't go to your place. We'll go to _____ place. (I, he, we, they, she)

7b. Write the pronoun that is specified by the terms. Usually only one pronoun is possible for each exercise. Consult the pronoun tables when you need to.

Example:

>First-person nominative singular: *I*
>Second-person possessive: *your, yours*
>Masculine third-person objective singular: *him*

>1. First-person objective singular:

>2. First-person objective plural:

>3. Second-person nominative singular (or plural):

>4. Feminine third-person nominative singular:

>5. Third-person nominative plural:

>6. Third-person objective singular (masculine):

>7. Third-person objective plural:

>8. First-person nominative plural:

>9. First-person possessive singular:

>10. Neuter third-person nominative singular:

7c. Classify the following pronouns according to person (first-, second-, or third-person), case (nominative, objective, or possessive), and number (singular or plural). With the third-person singular pronouns, also classify gender (masculine, feminine, or neuter). Consult the tables when necessary.

Examples:

I   (First-person nominative singular)
Me (First-person objective singular)

1. My

2. He

3. Him

4. Its

5. Yours

6. We

7. Us

8. Our

9. They

10. Them

7d. In the following sentences, identify and correct carelessly used pronouns. Some sentences may require some rewriting, and some of the underscored pronouns are correct. In some cases, there may be more than one way to rewrite the sentence.

1. If anyone sees a problem, <u>he</u> should report it immediately.

2. Neither excessive heat nor cold will damage the crop unless <u>they</u> last for weeks.

3. <u>Its</u> time to study grammar.

4. If <u>people</u> want to do well in this course, <u>you</u> should be prepared to work hard.

5. Each of these books has <u>their</u> correct place on the shelves.

6. Jim helped Jerry get to <u>his</u> apartment.

7. A medical doctor needs to know <u>her</u> science well.

8. Our dog has something in <u>it's</u> paw.

9. The tires need replacing and <u>it</u> needs a new transmission, but I only paid five hundred dollars for <u>it</u>.

10. As the bicyclists sped by the crowd, some of <u>them</u> nearly hit <u>them</u>.

7e. Complete the following tables for the simple tenses of the verb *to be*. Some subjects have been provided.

Simple tenses:

Singular	Present	Past	Future
1st person	I		
2nd person	You		
3rd person	He		

Plural	Present	Past	Future
1st person	We		
2nd person	You		
3rd person	They		

7f. Complete the following table for the perfect tenses of the verb *to be*. Also provide pronouns as subjects of the verbs.

Singular	Present	Past	Future
1st person			
2nd person			
3rd person			

7g. Complete the following tables for the progressive and perfect progressive tenses of the verb *to be*. Also provide pronouns as subjects of the verbs.

Progressive

Singular	Present	Past	Future
1st person			
2nd person			
3rd person			

Perfect Progressive

Singular	Present	Past	Future
1st person			
2nd person			
3rd person			

8 You Did *What?*

Verbs and Their Complements

In many sentences, **complements** are an important part of the predicate: They're called *complements* because they complete the verb.

For example, all these sentences are obviously incomplete:

Ralph seemed.
Alice gave.
Norton is.

The verbs here (*seemed*, *gave*, and *is*) each need another word (or more) to complete their meanings. They need complements. For example:

Ralph seemed <u>impatient</u>.
Alice gave <u>him</u> <u>his present</u>.
Norton is <u>their neighbor</u>.

The underlined words are **complements**—nouns, pronouns, or adjectives that complete the verb in some way and are part of the complete predicates of the sentences.

In this chapter, we'll examine five kinds of complements.

PREDICATE ADJECTIVES

Earlier we discussed two kinds of verbs: linking verbs and action verbs. We said that the relatively small number of linking verbs in English include *seem, become, appear, looked, felt,* and forms of the verb *to be.*

Linking verbs typically have complements. In these sentences, the complements are underlined:

Mr. Lochenhocher is irritable.
The staff appears efficient.
All of his sisters are musical.

Each of these underlined words is an adjective that follows the verb, and each describes the subject of the sentence. Such complements are called **predicate adjectives**. Here are some more examples:

This chapter looks easy.
He seems friendly.
They became calm and quiet.

PREDICATE NOMINATIVES

Predicate nominatives are nouns or pronouns that follow linking verbs and describe the subject. In these examples, the predicate nominatives are underlined:

George became President.
Helen was a teacher.
We are also teachers.

In each sentence, the noun phrase following the linking verb identifies the subject of the sentence. Here are more examples:

Ralph became <u>president of our club</u>.
Norton is <u>a menace</u>.
The Browns are <u>good neighbors and good citizens</u>.

Some grammar books call predicate nominatives *predicate nouns.* Still others combine predicate adjectives and predicate nominatives into a single category called *subject complements.*

Notice that sometimes the verb *be* is followed by an adverb, especially a prepositional phrase, instead of a complement:

Dad is <u>at the library</u>.
The kids are <u>in the car</u>.

DIRECT OBJECTS AND TRANSITIVE VERBS

We've discussed action verbs before, but here we learn a bit more about them.

There are two kinds of action verbs, **transitive** and **intransitive verbs.** Transitive verbs have complements; intransitive verbs don't need them. The sentences that follow contain intransitive verbs—no complement is present:

The accountant disappeared.
It rained today.
Rain fell all day.

Some intransitive verbs, like *disappeared,* typically don't take complements in any context.

Transitive verbs always have one or more complements, and they *must* have a **direct object**, a noun or pronoun that typically follows the verb and is the object of the verb's action in some way:

Susan saw <u>the Lloyds</u> at the mall.
June addressed <u>the audience</u>.
Ed baked <u>the cake</u> yesterday.

Here are more examples:

> Ed wrote <u>the article</u>.
> The newspaper published <u>the article and Ed's photos</u>.
> Mr. Lochenhocher wants <u>peace and quiet</u>.

Many verbs can be transitive or intransitive. That is, they can be used with or without direct objects:

Intransitive: I'll run to the store.
She read for two hours.
He laughed.
She sang.

Transitive: I run <u>the store</u>.
She read <u>the book</u>.
He laughed <u>a hearty laugh</u>.
She sang <u>an Irish song</u>.

When the direct object is a pronoun, it must be in the objective case:

> Susan saw <u>them</u> at the mall.
> Susan greeted <u>us</u> warmly.

INDIRECT OBJECTS

Indirect objects appear only in sentences with direct objects, and then they appear between the transitive verb and the direct object. They name a person or thing that receives the direct object in some way. In the following sentences, the indirect objects are underlined and the direct object is *a note*:

Bailey wrote <u>me</u> a note.
Ed wrote <u>her</u> a note.
We wrote <u>Bailey and Ed</u> a note.

Here are more sentences with indirect objects (underlined) followed by direct objects:

Mr. Redden taught <u>me</u> history.
Last night I read <u>my daughter</u> a book.
We bought <u>Ruthie</u> an accordion.

Notice that when pronouns are indirect objects, they are also in the objective case (as with *me* and *her* in the sentences above).

There is a test for the indirect object. Without changing the meaning of the sentence, the indirect object can be turned into the object of a prepositional phrase beginning with the preposition *to* or *for*. The prepositional phrase then appears *after* the direct object:

Mr. Redden taught history <u>to me</u>.
Last night I read a book <u>to my daughter</u>.
We bought an accordion <u>for Ruthie</u>.

But please notice the important difference. This sentence has an indirect object:

Mr. Redden taught <u>me</u> history.

The next sentence has no indirect object; *to me* is a prepositional phrase:

Mr. Redden taught history <u>to me</u>.

Some transitive verbs can take direct objects but cannot take indirect objects, as in these sentences:

Ned ate the cake.
Julie wanted cake.
Mr. Lochenhocher hates the violin.

OBJECT COMPLEMENTS

The **object complement** is the last kind of complement we'll discuss here, and it's another complement used only with a transitive verb and a direct object. Here are some examples:

We elected Bernice <u>president</u>.
We named Bob <u>the new treasurer</u>.
The news made Mr. Lochenhocher <u>angry</u>.

Object complements are nouns or adjectives that follow the direct object and describe the direct object, in roughly the same way that a predicate adjective or predicate nominative describes the subject.

With object complements, we don't distinguish between the adjectives and the nouns that describe the direct object—they are all object complements if they appear after the direct object and describe it.

Here are more examples:

We found the request <u>unreasonable</u>.
The Court declared the law <u>unconstitutional</u>.
The Court's decision renders the issue <u>null and void</u>.

It's important to distinguish object complements from other grammatical units. In the following pairs of sentences, the first sentence contains an object complement and the second sentence contains a different structure that is identified in the comment that follow:

They found Will <u>irritable</u>.
They found Will <u>at home</u>.
(*At home* is an adverbial prepositional phrase)

They made Bill <u>an officer</u>.
They made Bill <u>a cake</u>.
(In the second sentence, *Bill* is the indirect object; *cake* is a direct object.)

In everyday conversation, we often use the verbs *have and get* with object complements:

I have the car <u>ready</u>.
I will get the car <u>ready</u>.

Reflexive pronouns, the ones that end in *–self* (e.g., *himself, herself, themselves*) are often the direct objects that appear with object complements:

We got **ourselves** <u>ready</u>.
He imagined **himself** <u>successful</u>.

We'll discuss those pronouns in Chapter 19.

Object complements never appear in a clause that also contains an indirect object. They can only appear when there are direct objects in the same clause, and only a small number of transitive verbs can take object complements.

POINTS FOR WRITERS

As we've said, when we use a personal pronoun as a direct object or an indirect object, it has to be in the objective case. In these sentences, the underlined direct and indirect objects are objective case pronouns:

They gave <u>me</u> the job. (*Me* is the indirect object.)
We will find <u>her</u> immediately. (*Her* is the direct object.)
You must tell <u>them</u> the news. (*Them* is the indirect object.)
She has just informed <u>us</u>. (*Us* is the direct object.)

With predicate nominatives, which appear after linking verbs, the situation is a bit more complicated. Consider these versions of the same sentences:

The person responsible is <u>he</u>.
The person responsible is <u>him</u>.

It is <u>I</u>.
It is <u>me</u>.

Most of us would instinctively use the second version in each pair, because we're accustomed to using objective-case pronouns after a verb.

But the verb in these sentences, *is,* is a linking verb, and that makes *he* (and *him*) and *I* (and *me*) predicate nominatives. In the judgment of those writers and editors most careful about prescriptive grammar, we should use nominative case pronouns as predicate nominatives, because the pronoun is being equated with the subject: *It is I. It is he.* It is annoying.

Here again, the choices you make will depend on your editor, your audience, and the formality of your tone. It's often possible to rewrite the sentence to avoid the issue altogether.

EXERCISES

8a. In the following sentences, fill in the blanks with one word: *always, never,* or *sometimes.* (This is tougher than you might think. Feel free to look back at the chapter to work out the answers.)

1. Sentences with action verbs _____ have a complement.

2. Sentences with linking verbs _____ have a complement.

3. Sentences with intransitive verbs _____ have a complement.

4. Sentences with transitive verbs _____ have a complement.

5. Sentences with transitive verbs _____ have a direct object.

6. Sentences with transitive verbs _____ have an indirect object.

7. Sentences with linking verbs _____ have a predicate nominative.

8. Sentences with transitive verbs _____ have a predicate adjective.

9. Sentences with linking verbs _____ have a predicate adjective.

10. Sentences with transitive verbs _____ have an object complement.

11. Sentences with linking verbs _____ have an object complement.

12. Sentences with linking verbs _____ have a direct object.

8b. In the sentences below, identify the complements and classify them as a direct object, an indirect object, a predicate adjective, a predicate nominative, or an object complement. These simple sentences may have as many as two complements, but never more than two.

In some sentences, the complements are underlined. In others, there are no complements.

1. My daughter made me proud.

2. My aunt brought me a souvenir.

3. My sister is late.

4. Both my sisters are teachers.

5. Both my sisters are arriving at noon.

6. Six hours a day, Ruthie practices the accordion.

7. Ruthie practices for hours every day.

8. We sent Bill and Sue a gift.

9. They were kind and grateful.

10. I will address that issue at another time.

11. That fellow became our assistant.

12. Bonnie bought Ed that painting.

8c. Now go back through the sentences above and identify the verbs as linking, transitive, or intransitive.

9

All Together Now

Conjunctions, Compounds, and Subordinate Clauses

Like prepositions, conjunctions are connecting words. Broadly defined, **conjunctions** join one word or group of words with a similar word or group of words. There are two kinds.

COORDINATING CONJUNCTIONS

Coordinating conjunctions create **compound structures**: They connect two or more grammatically equivalent units of language: a word with a word, a phrase with a phrase, or one sentence with another sentence. In the below sentences, *and* is the coordinating conjunction:

I gave him <u>time and money</u>. (noun **and** noun)
I gave <u>promptly and generously</u>. (adverb **and** adverb)
The <u>white and blue</u> car is there. (adjective **and** adjective)
We <u>saw Ed and told him the news</u>. (predicate **and** predicate)

Here are a few sentences with compound subjects. The conjunctions (*and* and *or*) are in bold, and one of the sentences contains a three-part compound subject:

<u>You or I</u> have to clean up this mess.

Mark Twain, Damon Runyon, and J.R.R. Tolkien are three of Sam's favorite authors.

All the king's horses and all the king's men are having egg sandwiches.

These sentences contain compound verbs:

We hiked, swam **and** sailed until dark.

You can behave **or** leave.

I will sit **and** think **and** write all afternoon.

Here are sentences with compound prepositional phrases:

We can't find the dog in the house **or** in the yard.

In the spring, through the summer, **and** into the fall, we work in the garden.

You can combine any of these structures into a single sentence, using (for example) a compound subject, a compound verb, and a compound predicate:

Jim **and** Sue planned **and** prepared the meal **and** cleaned up afterward.

All the compound structures above depend on just two coordinating conjunctions: *and* and *or*. In fact, there are only seven coordinating conjunctions in English, so it's convenient to memorize them:

for	but
and	or
nor	yet
	so

There's a well-known mnemonic (a memory trick) for remembering these conjunctions: The first letters of these seven words spell the word *FANBOYS*.

THE CLAUSE AND THE COMPOUND SENTENCE

Now we come to one of the most important terms in grammar: the clause. For our purposes in this chapter, we'll use this definition:

> A **clause** is a unit of language that contains one subject and one predicate.

And *yes*, that definition sounds a good deal like our earlier tentative definition of a sentence. There's overlap between the two definitions for a simple reason: Any complete sentence contains at least one clause.

The seven coordinating conjunctions (the FANBOYS conjunctions) can join two or more clauses to create a larger structure called a **compound sentence**. To make the compound sentence, we select the conjunction that best communicates the relationship between the two clauses.

For example, each of the following is a complete sentence and also a single clause:

You will have to behave yourself.
You will have to leave.

With a coordinating conjunction, we can combine these two sentences into one sentence that contains two clauses:

You will have to behave yourself, **or** you will have to leave.

The following are more compound sentences, made by combining two clauses—the last sentence contains *three* clauses—all joined by coordinating conjunctions:

You have to leave, **for** you are not behaving yourself.

You are not behaving yourself, **so** you will have to leave.

Now you're behaving, **but** you have to leave anyway.

You're behaving now, **yet** you have to leave, **and** you can't come back.

(You'd be amazed how often people say things like that to grammar teachers.)

The coordinating conjunction *nor,* when used to construct a compound sentence, is a bit unusual: It requires a negative word (such as *not*) in the first clause, and it often requires a special word order in the second clause. *Nor* makes an auxiliary verb move to a position before the subject:

We do not want you to stay, **nor** do we want you to return.
You may not stay, **nor** may you return.

In these examples, *nor* makes the auxiliaries *do* and *may* shift to the left of the subjects (*we* and *you*).

CORRELATIVE COORDINATING CONJUNCTIONS

Correlatives are a special subclass of coordinating conjunctions. There are only four:

Either . . . or
Neither . . . nor
Both . . . and
Not only . . . but also

As you see, these **correlative coordinating conjunctions** consist of two parts, and the second part always contains one of the FANBOYS conjunctions: *or, nor, and,* or *but.* You've probably used them many times:

<u>Either Fred or George</u> should clean up their mess.
<u>Neither Fred nor George</u> cleaned up their mess.
<u>Both Fred and George</u> are jerks.
Fred and George are <u>not only jerks, but also idiots</u>.

(Correlative conjunctions are *very* useful.) The correlatives work in other compound structures, like compound predicates:

Fred and George **both** need to straighten up **and** fly right.

And *either . . . or* can join clauses to make compound sentences:

Either Fred and George must behave, **or** they must go.

Use *not only . . . but also* carefully. Inexperienced writers use the structure too often, or in ways that seem to imply that the first part of the compound structure is less important than the second portion. The writer may not intend to suggest that in these sentences:

She is <u>not only</u> a physician, <u>but also</u> a classical violinist.
He is <u>not only</u> a Lutheran minister, <u>but also</u> a professional wrestler.

If we don't want to minimize the importance of being a physician or a minister, we should rewrite these sentences and leave out the *not only* part:

She is <u>both</u> a physician <u>and</u> a classical violinist.
He is a Lutheran minister, <u>and</u> he is <u>also</u> a professional wrestler.

The first sentence uses the correlative coordinating conjunction *both . . . also*. In the second sentence, *and* is simply a coordinating conjunction accompanied by the adverb *also*.

SUBORDINATING CONJUNCTIONS

The second group of conjunctions are the **subordinating conjunctions**, which are the larger group. (See what we did there? We used the comparative adjective.) There are about thirty or so.

These conjunctions are used to connect one clause to another to make a single longer sentence with two or more clauses. The new sentence has qualities that we don't find in the compound sentences created by coordinating conjunctions.

The subordinating conjunction always appears at the beginning of one of the clauses. The clause begun this way is a **subordinate clause**.

Lists of the subordinating conjunctions vary from one grammar book to another, but the following list is reasonably complete. These are the *one-word* subordinating conjunctions:

after	once	when
although	since	whenever
as	than	where
because	that	wherever
before	though	whereas
however	till	whether
if	unless	while
lest	until	

The following sentences each contain one subordinate clause; the conjunction is in bold:

He left **because** he wanted to leave.
I'll go **when** I'm ready.
We'll let you know **if** she calls.
I will find you **wherever** you go.

Subordinate clauses are always adverbial, and they typically modify the verb, so they can often be moved around the sentence. They can be placed at the beginning or the end of the sentence:

Because he wanted to leave, he left.
When I'm ready, I'll go.
If she calls, we'll let you know.
Wherever you go, I will find you.

Notice that you can't do the same thing with clauses joined by coordinating conjunctions. You can certainly use a coordinating conjunction to join two independent clauses:

He was ready to leave, so he left.

But you can't move the second clause (including the conjunction) to the beginning of the sentence:

WRONG: <u>So he left</u>, he was ready to leave.

The movability of subordinate clauses is a useful feature. It helps us identify them, and it gives writers more stylistic options in constructing sentences.

In some cases, it's also possible to move the subordinate clause to the middle of the other clause, like this:

Fred and George, <u>because they are idiots</u>, are no longer welcome here.

Notice that in these cases, the subordinate clause is typically enclosed by a pair of commas. This placement of the subordinate clause, because it is unusual, is *emphatic*, so use it carefully.

Some subordinating conjunctions are more than one word: *as if, as though*, *so that*.

You should act **as if** you know what you're doing.
You should speak **as though** you know what you're talking about.
He took the job **so that** he could include it on his résumé.

Though these clauses modify the verb, they are not moveable.

Some grammars include *even though* among the subordinate conjunctions, as in *We're mentioning this* <u>even though</u> *you've probably had enough conjunctions*. An *even though* clause is generally moveable.

THAT DARNED *THAT*

One of the most troublesome subordinating conjunctions in the list above is *that*. It's not complicated, but *that* is used in many different ways, not just as a conjunction. We'll look at those uses in future chapters.

For now, consider these subordinate *that* clauses, and notice that they are all adverbial, but not moveable.

I am confident that I will win.
I am happy that you can be with us.
We were sad that you lost.

These clauses are adverbial but not because they modify the verb. Instead, they modify the adjectives (*confident, happy, sad*) in each sentence.

MORE CORRELATIVES

There are also **correlative subordinating conjunctions**:

as . . . as
so . . . that
the . . . the

We use these pairs of words to create adverbial clauses modifying only adverbs or adjectives. In the following sentence, the subordinate clause modifies adverbs:

I'll be there as soon as I can. (Modifying *soon*.)
They traveled as far as they could. (Modifying *far*.)

The *as . . . as* correlative can modify many adverbs (e.g., *as long as, as quickly as, as surely as*) and adjectives—*as many as* you like.

Here are examples of *so . . . that*, modifying adjectives:

He was so impatient that he slammed the door. (Modifying *impatient*.)

We were <u>so</u> weary <u>that we slept all afternoon</u>.
(Modifying *weary*.)

The strangest conjunction of all is surely *the . . . the*, based on the occasional adverbial use of *the* (as in *He is the worse for wear*):

<u>The</u> more he does that, <u>the less I like him</u>.
(Modifying the adverb *more*)

<u>The</u> bigger they are, <u>the faster I run</u>.
(Modifying the adjective *bigger*)

These subordinate clauses are *not* moveable.

DISTINGUISHING CONJUNCTIONS FROM PREPOSITIONS

A few conjunctions are identical to prepositions. The only way to distinguish these prepositions from the identical conjunctions is the context: If the word in question is followed by a clause, it's a conjunction. If the word in question is followed by a noun phrase or a pronoun, it's a preposition.

Prepositions that resemble coordinating conjunctions are *but* (meaning *except*) and *for*:

Preposition: No one can go <u>but</u> her.
                I brought the gift <u>for</u> this child.

Conjunction: He left, <u>but</u> he came back.
                He left, <u>for</u> it was late.

Some prepositions also resemble subordinating conjunctions, like *before, after, until, since,* and *as*:

Preposition: Come back <u>before</u> [or <u>after</u>] sunset.
              Don't come back <u>until</u> nine.
              He hasn't come back <u>since</u> nine.
              He is known <u>as</u> Jim.

Conjunction: Come back <u>before</u> [*or* <u>after</u>] Jim returns.
              He does that <u>until</u> he falls down.
              He hasn't come back <u>since</u> he graduated.
              He juggles <u>as</u> he rides a unicycle.

In every case, a noun follows the preposition and a clause follows the conjunction.

TWO KINDS OF CLAUSES

The conjunctions we've been examining require us to work with two different kinds of clauses, and now we need to make the distinction clear:

An **independent clause** contains at least one subject and at least one predicate, and it contains no word that makes the clause dependent on another clause to be complete. That is, it contains no word like a subordinating conjunction. An independent clause is grammatically complete by itself, without the addition of other clauses, so it can stand by itself as a complete sentence. When you encounter the term *main clause*, that's simply another term for an independent clause.

When we combine two or more independent clauses with a coordinating conjunction, we've created a compound sentence.

A **dependent clause** contains at least one subject and at least one predicate, and it is not grammatically complete by itself. When a dependent clause appears in a sentence, it functions as part of an independent clause.

According to these definitions, this is an independent clause:

We went to the museum.

But if we add a subordinating conjunction to it, it's a dependent clause that needs to be connected to another clause:

After we went to the museum . . .

One kind of dependent clause is a subordinate clause. It contains at least one subject and one predicate and it's connected to an independent clause by a subordinating conjunction. As you know by now, the example clause above (*After we went to the museum . . .*) is a subordinate clause.

Notice the difference between dependent clauses and subordinate clauses: Subordinate clauses are *one subcategory* of dependent clauses. This is a distinction that some grammar books, language textbooks, and dictionaries don't make.

We'll learn about other kinds of dependent clauses in the next few chapters.

ELLIPTICAL CLAUSES

In all kinds of ways, English sentences can contain **elliptical clauses**, sentences that often leave out words that are implied in context, as in [*You must*] *Get out!* Questions are also sometimes elliptical: *Why me?* (That is, *Why* [*do these things happen to*] *me?*) Elliptical structures help writers write concisely: *You are more ambitious than I* [*am*].

In elliptical clauses, we simply omit certain words that we need grammatically because they are—*in that particular context*—clearly implied. The missing words are often said to be *understood*; that is, the reader understands that certain words have been omitted for brevity.

When we're analyzing an elliptical clause, we insert the missing words because they're necessary for the grammatical completeness of the sentence, though the meaning of the sentence is clear without them.

Here are some examples, all well-known proverbs:

When in doubt, punt. (John Heismann)
When in doubt, don't. (Benjamin Franklin)
When in doubt, tell the truth. (Mark Twain)

If we rewrote these by making the implicit words explicit, they might read like this:

When [you are] in doubt, [you should] punt.
When [you are] in doubt, [you] don't [do what you were considering].
When [you are] in doubt, [you should] tell the truth.

Elliptical clauses are *not* fragment sentences, though they are often missing subjects, or part of their predicates:

We are going, [whether you] like it or not.
Whatever the situation [may be], he is uncooperative.
If [it is] necessary, we will speak to him.
[Money is] here today, [and] gone tomorrow.

In the following examples, the subject in the subordinate clauses is missing, but it is similar or identical to the subject in the independent clauses:

While [we were] looking for your book, we found your lost keys.
When [you are] traveling, you must keep your belongings secure.
She likes him better than [she likes] me.

The correlative subordinating conjunction *as . . . as* can create similar elliptical structures:

<u>She likes</u> him as much as [<u>she likes</u>] me.
He <u>dances</u> as well as she [<u>dances</u>].

And now [we'll have] one more [elliptical sentence] for the road, from J. K. Rowling:

When in doubt, go to the library.

POINTS FOR WRITERS

1. Variations on compound structures.

Sometimes writers choose to omit the conjunction (usually *and*) from compound structures. Carefully used, this unusual practice can make the compound structures more emphatic. Consider these series of compounds:

This project will require hard work, unwavering attention, total dedication.

". . . government of the people, by the people, for the people, shall not perish from the earth."

Be warned: If you overuse this variation, it ceases to be effective and, instead, becomes distracting or even pointless.

Another variation is to use the conjunction *and* to join each part of a compound structure with the next part, to emphasize that all the parts are of equal importance:

This project will require hard work **and** unwavering attention **and** total dedication.

Again, don't overuse this pattern.

Sometimes, when we have several compound sentences, we can improve sentence variety by omitting the conjunction in a two-clause sentence and replacing it with a semicolon:

> Luis excels at school, **for** he devotes many hours every week to studying.
> Luis excels at school; he devotes many hours every week to studying.

You've probably noticed in your reading that just one coordinating conjunction can create a compound sentence of three, four, or more independent clauses:

> A single coordinating conjunction can unite a sentence of two clauses, it can create a sentence of three or four clauses, **and** in rare cases it is used in a sentence of five clauses or more.

2. Compound subjects and verb agreement.

Compound subjects take singular or plural verbs, depending on the conjunction or, in some cases, the right-most subject. Look at these three examples:

> Bob **and** Ray are here.
> Either Bob **or** Ray is your assistant.
> Either Bob or the twins are your assistants.

The *and* in the first example means that the subject, *Bob and Ray*, is plural, so you need a plural verb: *are*.

The *or* in the second example means that the subject, *Bob or Ray*, is singular—*either Bob* **or** *Ray*—so you need the singular verb: *is*.

In the third example, the plural subject, *twins*, is the subject closest to the verb. In this case, you need the plural verb, *are*. If the compound subject were reversed—*either the twins* **or** *Bob*—the verb would be singular: *is*.

So the third example is grammatically correct, but it sounds awkward to many readers. We can usually improve a sentence like this by rewriting it:

BETTER: **Either** Bob **or** the twins will assist you.

3. So that.

In casual conversation and writing, we often use *so* by itself as an intensifier before an adjective or adverb to mean *very* or *really*:

He was <u>so</u> angry.
She ran <u>so</u> fast.

In formal writing and speaking, this is often regarded as a mistake, because *so*, used this way, requires a *that* clause to finish the idea:

He was <u>so</u> angry <u>that</u> he couldn't speak.
She ran <u>so</u> fast <u>that</u> she outdistanced all the other runners.

The *that* clause enables us to clarify how angry he was, or how fast she was. When we leave it out, we've failed to finish the idea.

Write *so* carefully *that* no one can accuse you of carelessness—unless you're deliberately seeking a casual, more conversational style.

4. Conjunctive adverbs.

We often use the following phrases in our reading, writing, and speaking:

therefore	however
moreover	nevertheless
thus	hence
indeed	in fact
likewise	in contrast

These phrases and many like them (e.g., *after all, as a result, consequently, furthermore, instead, meanwhile, on the contrary, still, then*) indicate some connection between the clauses they appear in and previous clauses:

She has been late three times this week; <u>therefore</u>, I don't consider her reliable.
He has been late three times this week; <u>however</u>, he is usually reliable.

These are **conjunctive adverbs**: They are adverbs that vaguely resemble conjunctions, because they indicate a relationship between the ideas of two clauses. But they are *not* conjunctions. They can't—by themselves—join the two clauses into a compound or complex sentence. That is, the connection indicated by conjunctive adverbs is one of ideas, not grammatical structure.

They are sometimes called *transitional adverbs*, and we use them to build paragraph coherence by signaling the connections among the sentences.

This affects punctuation. Notice the use of semi-colons—not commas—above. In each example, we could use periods instead of semi-colons and make two separate sentences. In that case, the second sentence in each example could still contain the conjunctive adverbs.

We can tell that these words are adverbs and not conjunctions because they are moveable in many contexts:

He has been late three times this week; <u>however</u>, he is usually reliable.

He has been late three times this week; he is, <u>however</u>, usually reliable.

We can't move a true conjunction around in its clause as we can move these conjunctive adverbs. If *however* were a true subordinating conjunction, it would have to remain at the beginning of the clause it introduces.

Notice that in the second example above, the placement of *however* after *is* creates a pause that gives greater emphasis to the next words, *usually reliable*.

In other words, conjunctive adverbs have at least two stylistic uses: to indicate transition from one idea to the next, and (if carefully used) to emphasis words that follow the adverbs.

However is sometimes used as an adverb in ways that are not conjunctive, such as an adverb modifying an adjective or adverb. In each of the cases below, the adjective or adverb in bold modifies a noun or verb before it (*fine, children,* or *to run*):

You must pay the fine, <u>however</u> **unreasonable**.
School children, <u>however</u> **young**, can learn responsibility.
She decided to run in the race, <u>however</u> **slowly**.

We can also use *however* as a subordinating conjunction, which is why it's in the list of conjunctions in this chapter:

We can rearrange this office <u>however</u> we wish.
Apparently you can use *however* <u>however</u> you like.

These clauses are not moveable.

5. Compounds and concise writing.

Compound structures help us achieve brevity in our writing. For example, with compounding, we can make one adjective modify several nouns:

> In the trunk in the attic, we discovered <u>old clothes, books, and photographs</u>.

Or we can use one preposition to apply to several objects, or one adverb to apply to several verbs:

> Mr. Benny is traveling **to** <u>Anaheim, Azusa, and Cucamonga</u>. We all <u>eagerly dressed, packed, and departed.</u>

6. Subtract the plus.

In your careful writing, don't use *plus* as a replacement for *and* unless your context is mathematical, or metaphorically mathematical:

> Hard work <u>plus</u> determination equal success.

EXERCISES

9a. Try to write, from memory, the seven coordinating conjunctions. (A hint: Remember *FANBOYS*.) Check your answers with the list in this chapter.

9b. Try to write, from memory, the four correlative coordinating conjunctions. Check your answers with the list in this chapter.

9c. Try to write, from memory, ten of the subordinating conjunctions, and consult the chapter to check your answers.

9d. In the following sentences, underline and classify the conjunctions as coordinating (C) or subordinating (S) and put brackets around any prepositions. Refer to the lists in this chapter and the previous chapter if you need to. Classify correlative conjunctions as coordinating.

Here's an example:

[In] the following sentences, underline <u>and</u> (C) classify the conjunctions [as] coordinating <u>or</u> (C) subordinating <u>and</u> (C) put brackets [around] any prepositions.

1. The film was not only boring, but also offensive, so we asked for a refund and went home.

2. In the morning and again in the evening, Ruthie practices her violin until her mother can't stand it anymore.

3. We went to the diner for lunch, for we were expected back soon.

4. Because we are tired, we'll take a short break before we continue studying.

5. Fred and George have been gone since Friday night, since they took a "short break" from studying.

6. After I finish this project, we can meet after work and discuss the project.

7. Fred and George are neither punctual nor organized, yet they somehow do their work well.

8. He was so confident that he underestimated his opponent.

9. The room looked as if it had not been occupied in some time, but it had been occupied for days or weeks.

10. The longer he waited, the more impatient he became.

9e. In the following sentences, identify and label compound subjects, compound verbs, compound predicates, and other compound structures, but not clauses. There are no compound sentences. Not every sentence contains a compound.

1. Anne always fastens her seatbelt and locks her doors before she drives.

2. Anne and James are driving to Nashville and Chattanooga.

3. In Nashville, Anne shopped and visited her family.

4. She and I always enjoy Nashville, but seldom go there.

5. The next day we will drive from Tennessee to Illinois.

6. In Illinois, we will visit the Lincoln Museum and the Lincoln Library.

7. We will stop in Wisconsin or Minnesota for the night.

8. In Minnesota we will ski and visit family.

9. Anne and her sister Alice love skiing.

10. In cold weather, James stays indoors and reads.

10 Sentencing Guidelines

Building Sentences with Clauses

Previously, we've learned about conjunctions that join one clause to another. Now we can finally define some of the most important terms in grammar regarding clauses and sentences, and the subject is important enough that it merits a bit of repetition.

As we've learned before, a **clause** is a unit of language that contains one subject and one predicate. That definition overlaps with our working definition of a sentence because every sentence contains at least one clause.

We've said that are two general kinds of clauses in English:

An **independent clause** contains one subject and one predicate, and it contains no word that makes the clause dependent on another clause to be complete. That is, it contains no word like a subordinating conjunction or others that we will learn about. An independent clause is grammatically complete by itself, so it can stand by itself as a complete sentence.

A **dependent clause** contains one subject and one predicate, and it is not grammatically complete by itself. It functions as part of an independent clause. Dependent clauses include the subordinate clause (which we create with a subordinating conjunction), and other kinds of dependent clauses that we'll learn about soon.

According to these definitions, this is an independent clause:

We fixed dinner for our parents last night.

But if we add a subordinating conjunction to it, it becomes a dependent clause that needs to be connected to an independent clause:

<u>Before</u> we fixed dinner for our parents last night . . .

A subordinate clause is one kind of dependent clause. A subordinate clause contains one subject and one predicate, and it must be connected to an independent clause by a subordinating conjunction. The clause above (*Before we fixed dinner* . . .) is a subordinate clause.

Again, notice the difference between dependent clauses and subordinate clauses: A subordinate clause is one kind of dependent clause. (We'll study two other kinds of dependent clauses in later chapters: the **relative clause** and the **nominal clause**.)

Finally, here is a new definition of a sentence, that important unit of language that we've talked about all along:

A **sentence** is a unit of language that contains at least one independent clause. It may also contain one or more dependent clauses.

Like most definitions of a sentence, this one would not satisfy most linguists (a notoriously argumentative bunch), but it will do for our purposes.

CLASSIFYING BY STRUCTURE

With these definitions, we go on to the well-known, four-part classification of sentences, based on their structures:

- Simple sentences
- Compound sentences
- Complex sentences
- Compound-Complex sentences

You've probably encountered them before:

Simple Sentence: A simple sentence contains only one independent clause:

I went to the garage.

A simple sentence can contain a compound subject, a compound predicate, or other compound structures. The sentence below contains one compound subject and one compound predicate, so it's still a simple sentence:

Alphonse **and** I went to the garage, found his car, **and** drove it home.

The following sentence contains a compound subject, a compound verb, and a compound predicate:

Jim **and** Louise planned **and** prepared the meal **and** cleared up afterward.

It's still just one clause, so it's a simple sentence.

Compound Sentence: A compound sentence contains at least two clauses: two or more independent clauses joined by one or more coordinating conjunctions. There are no dependent clauses in a compound sentence:

I went to the garage, **and** I found my bike.

I found my bike, **but** the tires were flat.

Complex Sentence: A complex sentence contains at least two clauses: only one independent clause and one or more dependent clauses. In the examples in this chapter, the dependent clauses will be joined to the independent clauses by one or more subordinating conjunctions (shown in bold):

I went to the garage **because** I needed my bike.

Complex sentences can also contain relative clauses or nominal clauses, as we will soon see.

Compound-Complex Sentence: A compound-complex sentence contains at least three clauses. It contains two or more independent clauses joined by one or more coordinating conjunctions, and it also contains one or more dependent clauses. In the example below, the dependent clause is a subordinate clause, joined by a subordinating conjunction:

I went to the garage **because** I needed my bike, **and** I found it.

As we'll soon see, compound-complex sentences can also contain relative clauses or nominal clauses.

Fragments: There's a fifth kind of sentence that's not really a sentence at all. It's a **fragment sentence**, a structurally incomplete sentence, and there are many ways to write them. Here's one way:

I went to the garage **and** I found my bike. <u>**Because** I needed it</u>.

The second sentence is a fragment; it's simply a subordinate clause that is punctuated like a sentence. We use such fragments all the time in conversation:

Why were you looking for your bike?
<u>Because I needed it</u>.

Usually no one objects, or even notices. In careful writing, however, we should avoid fragments unless we're deliberately using them for emphasis. Even then, we should use them with restraint.

What if we combine two fragments? Do two fragments make a whole? The following consists of two subordinate clauses, punctuated like a complete sentence:

When he finally arrives, if the plane is on time.

Combining two (or more) dependent clauses still makes a fragment sentence, because a sentence has to have at least one independent clause. This kind of fragment is never acceptable, unless you're Gertrude Stein, and you probably aren't. (If you *are*, get in touch with us immediately.)

CLASSIFYING BY PURPOSE

There is another way to classify sentences: according to their purposes. Even in these classifications, sentence structure and punctuation are important.

As we've seen, **declarative sentences** make a statement. They usually have the *subject + predicate* structure we've examined (subject first, predicate second), and they usually end with a period:

I am in trouble.

Interrogative sentences ask a question. They may begin with a question word (*Who? What? When? Where? Why? How?*) or with a verb. They typically end with a question mark:

<u>Why</u> do these things always happen to me?

<u>How</u> can these things keep happening?
<u>Do</u> things like this ever happen to you?

As the third example above shows, many questions (those that can be answered by *yes* or *no*) can be formed from declarative sentences by altering the placement of a verb. An auxiliary verb (like *do*) is placed before the subject:

You know what I'm talking about.
<u>Do</u> you know what I'm talking about?

Sometimes, especially in conversation and fictional dialogue, interrogatives are just a word or two that make sense in context (we hope):

What? Why?
Who, me?

Interrogatives can also be statements that end in tag questions:

You did forget your textbooks, <u>didn't you</u>?
I won't need them, <u>will I</u>?

These two examples above are not run-on sentences or comma splices. They are correct, completely acceptable sentences, and they're a bit more complicated than they might look.

As you see in the two examples, a **tag question** is added to the end of a declarative sentence with a comma, and it repeats the auxiliary verb and the subject of the declarative. If the declarative is positive (*You did forget your textbooks*), the tag question is negative (*didn't you?*). If the declarative is negative (*I won't need them*), the tag is positive (*will I?*).

In other words, negative tag questions anticipate positive answers:

You forgot your textbooks, didn't you?
Oh—yes, I did.

And positive tag questions anticipate negative answers:

I won't need them, will I?
No, you won't.

But we don't always get the answer we anticipate, do we? (Or, as the great Fats Waller often said: "One never knows, *do* one?")

An **imperative sentence** is a command. It may end with a period or an exclamation mark, and it may be missing the subject:

Get out of here!
Go!
Scram!
Get lost!

In an imperative sentence, the missing subject is often an implied second-person pronoun (*you*) perhaps with an implied auxiliary verb:

[You must] Get out of here!
[You must] Stop that!

Commands can be phrased more politely, but they're still imperatives:

Please don't do that.

Exclamatory sentences express strong emotion. They have no distinctive structure or end punctuation, and they're often incomplete sentences or just a phrase:

No!
Don't!
Oh, that's just *great*
What the heck?

The four classifications that we just examined illustrate how inadequate simple terms and concepts sometimes are in analyzing what language can do. In some cases, because language is capable of explicit and implicit meanings, sentences don't clearly fit in any single category; they may have implicit meanings quite different from their explicit purpose.

Suppose a teacher in a classroom says to a student,

You look puzzled.

In that context, this declarative sentence may contain an implicit interrogative: *Do you have a question?*

Or suppose the teacher says to a student in the back row,

I'm watching you.

That could be an implicit imperative, meaning *Stop what you're doing! Behave yourself!*

The teacher might imply the same imperative idea with a question: *Did you have something to say?*

POINTS FOR WRITERS

1. Beginning sentences with conjunctions.

You may have learned in school that writers should not begin a sentence with the subordinating conjunction *because*, like this:

Because Linda was late for school, she left home hastily.

In fact, that is a perfectly good complex sentence, and good writers do indeed begin sentences with *because*. But you shouldn't do this:

WRONG: Because Linda was late for school. She left home hastily.

As we saw earlier, a subordinate clause has to be connected to an independent clause unless you're deliberately writing a fragment.

You can also begin sentences with coordinating conjunctions, but don't overdo it. We've done it twice in the last page or so:

But you shouldn't do this.
And, even then, we should use them with restraint.

The initial conjunction connects the idea of the sentence to the preceding sentences—it's one way to create **paragraph coherence**. It also contributes to a somewhat less formal tone, which is desirable in some contexts.

A sentence that begins with a coordinating conjunction is not a fragment sentence. It is a stylistic variation that you should use with restraint.

2. Commas in compound structures.

When a sentence contains a compound phrase of two parts, commas are usually not necessary:

My brother and your sister are planning a party.

When there are three or more parts in the compound structure, we typically use only one conjunction to join them all, and commas separate the parts:

My brother, your sister, **and** their friends are planning a party.

As you may have noticed in the examples earlier, compound sentences use a comma to mark the end of every independent clause except the last:

Now you're behaving yourself, **but** you have to leave anyway.

You're behaving yourself now, **yet** you have to leave, **and** you can't come back.

When the two clauses are short and simple, we can omit the comma:

I am angry and I am leaving.

When the clauses are long and complex, the commas separating the clauses become more important. They help the reader understand where one clause begins and another ends.

When a subordinate clause begins the sentence, the comma separates the subordinate clause from the independent clause, unless the subordinate clause is brief and the sentence is unambiguous without the comma:

Because I could not stop for Death, I hid behind a tree. (Emily Dickinson, improved.)

The sentences below challenge our comprehension (at least a little) because they each need a comma to mark the end of a subordinate clause. Read these sentences and decide where the commas should go:

Because you've already eaten dinner at our house tonight will be postponed.

After you've eaten the dog should be fed right away.

Yes, we *deliberately* wrote these sentences to be difficult without the comma. But such sentences do occur in our everyday writing. Commas are important in these cases because they clarify the structure of the sentence for the reader. (If you haven't yet worked it out, both of those last two examples need a comma after *eaten*.)

EXERCISES

10a. Go back to the beginning pages of this chapter and reread the definitions of an independent clause, a dependent clause, and a sentence. Then try to write the three definitions from memory, and use the book to check your work.

10b. Classify the following sentences according to their structures. Each sentence will be simple, compound, complex, or compound-complex. Refer to the definitions in this chapter when you need to.

Here are a few points to help you:

- Pay attention to punctuation, which often helps.
- Watch for conjunctions of all kinds; don't confuse prepositions with conjunctions.
- Remember that a compound phrase of some sort (like a compound subject or compound direct object) may be in a sentence that does not itself have compound structure.

Finally, there is at least one fragment sentence here that can't be classified any other way. Classify every incomplete sentence you find as a fragment.

1. My family owned a cocker spaniel when I was young.

2. Before the meeting, we will set up the room, and you should prepare the refreshments.

3. Before the meeting begins, we will set up the room, and you should prepare the refreshments.

4. He has done well since graduation, and he credits his success to the university.

5. As if he is our supervisor.

6. Since graduation, when he began working here, while Arthur was the supervisor of both departments.

7. Louise and Sharon went to the garage and found their car.

8. Either Arthur and Gwyn find a way to solve this problem themselves, or they must seek help.

9. Both spring and fall are their favorite seasons for camping and fishing in the mountains.

10. We sat nervously as we waited for our interviews.

11. During our interviews, the applicants occasionally answered poorly, but in general they did well.

12. After they left the office, they returned, for Louise had forgotten her portfolio.

10c. Return to the sentences in **10b**, and identify the complete subjects and predicates in all the clauses of all the complete sentences. Put subjects in brackets and underline predicates.

10d. Classify the following sentences according to their purposes: Each sentence will be declarative, interrogative, imperative, or exclamatory. (Don't worry about possible implicit meanings.) Refer to the definitions in this chapter when you need to.

1. What a mess!

2. What are you shouting about?

3. I forgot my portfolio, and now the office is closed.

4. Just relax and get it tomorrow.

5. Listen!

6. The boys' choir is singing.

7. What music those children make!

8. Didn't Count Dracula say that once?

9. Are you comparing the boys' choir to wolves?

10. Stop twisting my words!

11 Relative Clauses, Which We Need

In this chapter we learn about another kind of dependent clause, the **relative clause**. There are two kinds of relative clauses. The first that we'll examine is based on the relative pronouns; the second is based on the relative adverbs.

THEY'RE *ALL* RELATIVE

The **relative pronouns** are

who
whom
whose
which
that

(*Whom* is the objective form of *who*; *whose* is the possessive.)

Committing these five relative pronouns to memory will help you recognize relative clauses.

As you'll see in the examples below, relative pronouns begin relative clauses. The relative clauses are underlined:

The man **who** spoke to you is my uncle.
My uncle is the man **whom** you saw.

The woman **whose** car you hit is my neighbor.
The car, **which** is a total wreck, is a Chevrolet.
The car **that** you hit is a Chevrolet.

Relative clauses modify nouns in a sentence. They cannot be moved around like subordinate clauses, but always appear after the nouns they modify.

Relative pronouns play two roles in a sentence. First, relative pronouns connect their own clause to another clause, which is usually independent. Second, as pronouns, they stand in for nouns. The relative pronoun appears in the relative clause, and the antecedent of the pronoun is in the independent clause.

Here's an important point: The antecedent of the relative pronoun is always the noun modified by the relative clause.

To examine relative clauses further (or even *farther*), let's begin with two brief independent clauses:

1. The job is part-time.
2. You want the job.

With a relative pronoun, we can replace the words *the job* in Sentence 2 with the relative pronoun *that* to create (with a bit of rearranging) a relative clause: *that you want*. Then we can embed that clause into the middle of Sentence 1:

            2.
1. The job **that** you want is part-time.

The words *that you want* make up the relative clause, which is now part of Sentence 1, the independent clause.

As you've just seen, with relative pronouns we can combine two independent clauses into one complex sentence. The resulting sentence has one independent clause and one relative clause embedded inside the independent clause. And, of course, the sentence may contain more than two clauses.

As the example above shows, the relative clause is adjectival: the relative clause modifies *job*. Relative clauses are always adjectival and always follow the nouns they modify.

The word order often changes in the relative clause because the relative pronoun must appear early in the clause.

Here's another example, using *who*. We'll begin with two independent clauses:

1. That man is my uncle.
2. That man talked to you.

Now, we use *who* to replace *that man* in Sentence 2. Then we embed the resulting relative clause into the middle of Sentence 1:

                 2.
1. That man **who** talked to you is my uncle.

Here's another example, using *whom*:

1. The man is my uncle.
2. You saw the man.

Again we replace *the man* in Sentence 2 with *whom*, move the relative pronoun to the beginning of the clause, and combine the clauses:

                 2.
1. The man **whom** you saw is my uncle.

Here are more sentences with relative clauses:

I got the job, **which** is part-time.
I borrowed the broom from the woman **whose** house I rent.

Relative pronouns can be the objects of prepositions. In that case, the relative pronoun appears just after the preposition in the relative clause:

There is the man <u>to **whom** you must speak</u>.

In all of these examples, and any others we might find, we see the same features of the relative clause built with relative pronouns:

1. The relative pronoun appears at or near the beginning of the relative clause.
2. In its clause, the relative pronoun stands in for the modified noun, which is always the antecedent of the relative pronoun.
3. The relative clause follows the antecedent—that is, it follows the modified noun. This means that relative clauses *cannot* appear at the beginning of a sentence, as subordinate clauses can, but only in the middle or at the end.

ADVERBS, RELATIVELY

There are just two **relative adverbs,** *when* and *where*, and, like the relative pronouns, they help us form relative clauses that are adjectival. Yes, it seems odd that an adverb is the basis of an adjectival clause, but wait and see.

The relative adverbs *when* and *where* are like relative pronouns in other ways: They seem to refer back to a noun earlier in the sentence, and they begin the clause they introduce.

We use *when* to begin a relative clause that modifies a noun that names times:

I have to finish this paper by noon, **when** <u>it is due</u>.
The year 1929, **when** <u>the stock market crashed</u>, is the subject of this new book.

In each case, the relative clauses are underlined, and *when* is an adverb in the relative clause. *When* refers to the time noun (*noon, the year 1929*) that is modified by the relative clause.

We use *where* in relative clauses that modify nouns that name places:

Her favorite city is Atlanta, **where** she was born.

Marshfield, Missouri, **where** astronomer Edwin Hubble grew up, is a pleasant little town.

In each sentence, the relative clause modifies the place word (*Atlanta* and *Marshfield, Missouri*) that precedes the relative adverb.

Here are some more examples:

This is a month **when** temperatures are low.

I know a store **where** we will find that book.

This is the time of year **when** days get shorter.

I know of a spooky abandoned house **where** ghosts, werewolves, and my old high school teachers have been seen.

(That last sentence is *not true*. There are no such things as werewolves.)

In this chapter, all the sentences containing relative clauses are complex sentences, with one independent clause and one dependent clause. But relative clauses can also appear in sentences with more clauses.

In sentences built with relative adverbs, we all find the same features:

1. The relative adverb appears at the beginning of the relative

clause.
2. The relative adverb is selected on the basis of the word that will be modified by the relative clause: *when* to modify time words, and *where* to modify place words.
3. The relative clause follows the modified word. This means that relative adverb clauses cannot appear at the beginning of a sentence, as subordinate clauses can, but only in the middle or at the end.

These features are noticeably similar to the features of the relative clauses built with pronouns. (You *did* notice that, didn't you? Didn't you?)

POINTS FOR WRITERS

1. Omitted relative adverbs.

Sometimes in casual writing and conversation, the relative adverbs *when* and *where* are left out:

This is the time of year <u>days get shorter.</u>
This is the month <u>temperatures are low</u>.
I know a place <u>we can find that new book</u>.

Generally ignored in conversation, these omissions sometimes seem odd in writing. Don't do this in your formal writing**.**

2. Restrictive and non-restrictive clauses.

Consider these two sentences, both of them containing the same relative clause. Do you see the differences in the meaning of these two sentences?

All politicians <u>who are crooks</u> should go to jail.

All politicians, who are crooks, should go to jail.

The commas make a big difference. In the first sentence, we're told that *only* those politicians who are crooks should go to jail.

In the second, we're told parenthetically that *all* politicians are crooks, and they *all* should go to the hoosegow.

We're comparing **restrictive** and **non-restrictive** relative clauses here. In the first sentence, the restrictive clause restricts the meaning of *all politicians* to include *only* those who are crooks. The non-restrictive clause in the second sentence informs us that all politicians are crooks.

The pair of commas in the second sentence (known as *parenthetical commas*) make the enclosed information supplemental, so that the relative clause does not modify or restrict the words *all politicians*.

Here are some more examples:

It's fun to watch magicians who are clever.
It's fun to watch magicians, who are clever.

The first sentence tells us that only some magicians (those who are clever) are fun. The second sentence gives us some supplementary information about *all* magicians.

Notice that the non-restrictive clauses could be enclosed in parentheses instead of commas.

In some sentences, the commas don't seem to make much difference:

I dislike those baseball fans who are rude.
I dislike those baseball fans, who are rude.

In both cases, we're speaking about a particular group of fans, although the first sentence seems to be about *all* rude fans; the second, about a *particular* group of rude fans.

3. Troublesome relatives.

Some grammar books include *why* among the relative adverbs:

> I know the reason **why** he left.

But sentences like this are considered redundant, because we can usually delete the modified noun (*reason*) without losing any information:

> I know **why** he left.

In this new sentence, *why he left* is not a relative clause, but a **nominal clause**, which we'll learn about in Chapter 12.

4. More troublesome relatives.

(You know, it's *hard* to avoid troublesome relatives.) Notice the ambiguous use of *which* in this sentence:

> The senator said he believed that the general will resign, and the newspaper published an editorial agreeing with what the senator said, **which** disappointed me.

Using pronouns near the end of long sentences can confuse readers, who may not be able to tell what the precise antecedent is. (In the example above, what does *which* refer to?) This is an important point because clarity is always important. Make sure antecedents are clear.

To improve a sentence like the one above, you may need to break it up into two or more sentences, and you certainly want to make clear *what* disappointed you:

> The senator disappointed me when he said . . .
> I was disappointed to hear that the general will resign . . .
> The newspaper editorial disappointed me when . . .

5. Who or that?

Compare these sentences:

I'll speak with the man <u>who</u> runs this place.
I'll speak with the man <u>that</u> runs this place.

We use both versions in informal communication, and few people notice or care. In formal writing, however, many writers and editors prefer to use only *who* (and *whom*) to refer to people.

6. Who or whom?

Because a relative pronoun always has a grammatical function in its relative clause, sometimes we have to decide when to use *who* or *whom*. *Who* is the nominative form of the pronoun, used for subjects; *whom* is the objective. Compare:

I'll speak with the man *who* runs this place.
That is the man with *whom* I spoke.

Writers and speakers are often uncertain about when to use *whom*, which may be one reason many people prefer *that* instead. Let's sort some matters out.

When the pronoun follows a preposition (as in the second example above), the grammatically correct choice is *whom*: *With whom I spoke.*

Sometimes rearranging the sentence, or part of it, makes the choice easier. If we're ending a sentence with a preposition (as in *He is the person who I spoke with*), putting the preposition before the pronoun makes it more obvious that we need the objective case:

He is the person <u>with whom</u> I spoke.

Suppose we have a question like this:

<u>Who</u> do you trust?

Who may sound right because we're accustomed to putting a nominative-case pronoun at the beginning of a sentence. But try to answer the question using either *he* or *him*:

I trust <u>him</u>.

The answer to the question is *him* (an objective case pronoun) because it's the direct object of *trust*. In the question above, the pronoun is also the direct object, so use *whom*:

<u>Whom</u> do you trust?

Try out the same procedures with these two questions:

Is that the man <u>who</u> danced with her?
Do you know the man <u>who</u> she danced with?

In the first case, it's possible to revise the relative clause into a sentence using *he* or *him* (*He danced with her*) which indicates that we need the nominative pronoun, *who*, in the question.

In the second example, rephrasing the sentence by moving the preposition gives us *Do you know the man <u>with who</u> she danced?* It's now obvious that we need *whom*:

Do you know the man <u>*whom*</u> she danced with?
Do you know the man <u>*with whom*</u> she danced?

In casual conversation, we'll all misuse *who* or *whom* sometimes. But in our formal professional writing, this is often a matter we want to get right—or that an editor or co-author wants right. The *he/him* test can help us work out these things.

In contexts in which you aim for a more conversational style, a more informal tone, using *who* instead of *whom* can contribute to that effect.

EXERCISES

11a. Underline the relative clauses in the following sentences. Double-underline the relative pronouns. Then locate the nouns modified by each relative clause and enclose them in square brackets, as in this example:

We took that bin of recyclables to the [agency] <u>that collects them</u>.

Remember that some uses of *that* are not relative pronouns. You'll see an example here.

1. The house that is being renovated was my grandmother's home.

2. Please get the book, which I left in my office.

3. You can give that letter to the man who is waiting outside.

4. The woman whose car you dented wants to speak to you.

5. The man who is waiting already has that letter that you left in your office.

6. The customer whom you phoned is waiting in the office.

7. I know the man to whom they spoke.

11b. Underline the relative clauses in the following sentences. Double-underline the relative adverbs. Locate the nouns modified by each relative clause and enclose them in square brackets, as in this example:

Yesterday my father drove by the [house] <u>where he was born.</u>

1. The house where he was born is on Fifth Street.

2. In April 1943, when he was born, his parents were living and working in the city.

3. Spring is the season when I am happiest, and home is the place where I am most comfortable.

4. Marceline, where young Walt Disney lived, is a small town in northern Missouri.

5. In 1911, when his family moved to Kansas City, Disney left Marceline.

11c. Rewrite each of the following pairs of sentences as a single sentence with a relative clause. Make the second sentence the relative clause.

Here's a hint: Find a noun phrase that appears in both sentences. Then replace the phrase in the second sentence with a relative pronoun that will begin the relative clause.

A reminder: The relative pronouns are *who, whom, whose, which,* and *that.*

After you've revised the sentence, underline the relative clause that you created.

Here's an example:

The dictionary could be helpful. You brought the dictionary. (Use *that*.)

REWRITE: The dictionary <u>that you brought</u> could be helpful.

1. That man is my neighbor. That man is standing over there. (Use *who* or *whom*.)

2. I like the car. You rented the car today. (Use *that*.)

3. The woman is at the door. You called the woman earlier. (Use *who* or *whom*.)

4. The dog has been found. I lost the dog. (Use *that*.)

5. My mother is watching *Casablanca*. My mother loves old movies. (Use *who* or *whom*.)

11d. Rewrite each pair of sentences as one sentence with a relative clause. Make the second sentence the relative clause. Underline the relative clause in each new sentence.

A hint: Find a noun phrase that appears in both sentences. Then replace the phrase in the second sentence with a relative adverb, either *where* or *when*, that will begin the relative clause. You may have to rearrange quite a few words in the new sentence. Here's an example:

The house is a century old. He lives in the house.

REWRITE: The house <u>where he lives</u> is a century old.

1. Gary, Indiana, is a pleasant small city. I was born in Gary, Indiana.

2. I walked down the street. She lives on the street.

3. Christmas is a wonderful time of year. Christmas is when

my entire family gathers together.

4. There is the hospital. I was born in the hospital.

5. The book is in the living room. Ron is reading in the living room.

12 I Know That You Know What They Are

Nominal Clauses

A **nominal clause**, another kind of dependent clause, can fill noun positions in a sentence. Nominal clauses enable us to embed a clause within a larger sentence and use the sentence to make some observation or judgment about the nominal clause.

Let's begin with these sentences, each of which has a transitive verb and a direct object:

I know <u>Bill</u>.
He knows <u>Oshkosh</u>.
She will know <u>the answer</u>.

Now, let's take this sentence:

The plane will leave on time.

We can make this sentence into a nominal clause to make a number of statements about the clause:

He knows <u>that the plane will leave on time</u>.
She will know <u>if the plane will leave on time</u>.
<u>Why the plane did not leave on time</u> is beyond my comprehension.

There are two kinds of nominal clauses, and we distinguish them here by the word that begins the clause.

QUESTION-WORD NOMINALS

These nominal clauses begin with the question words *who, what, when, where, why, how* and *which*. They can also begin with **compound pronouns**, the ones that begin with question words and end with *ever* (*whoever, whomever,* and *whatever*).

Let's begin with a question: *Who did it?* We can embed that question within a declarative sentence, as a direct object. Here the nominal clause is underlined:

I know **who** did it.

We can also create direct objects with other clauses that begin with question words:

I learned **what** he did.
I discovered **when** he did it.
I saw **where** he did it.
I will ask **why** he did it.
I will show you **how** he did it.

Notice that most of these nominal clauses are not worded like questions by our usual standards: They don't have the normal word order of questions.

The compound pronouns—*whoever, whomever,* and *whatever*—can also begin nominal clauses:

We will use **whatever** we find.
We will hire **whoever** applies for this job.

FILLING NOUN POSITIONS

As the examples above illustrate, nominal clauses appear where nouns can appear. They are often the direct objects of transitive verbs like *know, see,* and *learn.*

Nominal clauses can also be subjects:

Where these people went is not yet known.
Why they come here is a mystery.

Nominal clauses can be objects of a preposition:

The professor is writing a book about **how** people can improve their writing.

Mr. Chayle has time for **whoever** needs help and for **whatever** happens.

They can be indirect objects:

You can give **whoever** applies the job.

And they can be predicate nominatives, following linking verbs:

My question is **who** took my lunch?

NOMINALS WITH *THAT, IF,* OR *WHETHER*

The three words *that, if,* and *whether* (sometimes called **nominalizers**) can also make independent clauses into nominal clauses that fill noun positions. Here are nominal clauses functioning as direct objects:

I wonder **if** <u>she arrives today</u>.
I learned **that** <u>she arrives today</u>.
I don't know **whether** <u>[or not] she will arrive today</u>.
He demanded **that** <u>they serve him immediately</u>.
We doubt **if** <u>they will cooperate</u>.

In the third example above, *whether or not* could be treated as a single nominalizing phrase. The sentences above demonstrate that these nominal clauses can be direct objects of the verbs *know, see,* and *learn*. They could also be objects of the verbs *demand, ask, inquire, imagine, doubt,* and others.

These verbs indicate an intellectual process that is being performed upon the idea in the nominal clause. More simply, we're thinking about the idea of the nominal clause.

These clauses can perform almost every other function of a noun. They can be subjects:

> **That** <u>the sun is at the center of our solar system</u> is beyond all question.

These clauses can also perform other nominal functions, including those of predicate nominatives or objects of prepositions:

> The main complaint about the car was **that** <u>it was too expensive</u>.

> We know nothing about him except **that** <u>he arrived yesterday</u>.

We often omit the *that* nominalizer:

> The main complaint about the car was **[that]** <u>it was too expensive</u>.

> We know nothing about him except **[that]** <u>he arrived yesterday</u>.

But we can't omit *if* or *whether*:

> We asked **if they are ready**.

> We wondered **whether they were ready**.

In the exercises in this chapter, nominalized clauses will always make *that* explicit.

POINTS FOR WRITERS

1. That's that.

Compare these sentences:

> I know **that** he will attend the ceremony.
> I know he will attend the ceremony.

> We showed them **that** they were wrong.
> We showed them they were wrong.

In the first pair, the version without *that* is more conversational, more direct, and stronger. That's how we read it, anyway.

In the second pair, omitting *that* eliminates the clumsy series of three words beginning with *th-*. That's an especially helpful change if the text is to be read aloud.

Eliminating *that* would also help this sentence:

> We should tell them **that** that music is too loud.

You can see that that *that* before *that music* is so repetitive that that *that* should be deleted. And that's that.

I Know That You Know What They Are: Nominal Clauses | 145

EXERCISES

12a. In the following sentences, identify the functions of each underlined nominal clause. The clauses can be direct objects, subjects, indirect objects, object complements, predicate nominatives, or other functions.

1. I know <u>why you did that</u>.

2. I can't imagine <u>what they will do next</u> or <u>who will do it</u>.

3. <u>When they arrive</u> is unknown.

4. You already know <u>that they don't know the area well.</u>

5. <u>Why they come here</u> is a mystery.

6. The professor is writing a book about <u>how people improve their writing.</u>

7. <u>Whether he will succeed</u> is <u>what we are all wondering.</u>

8. He discussed <u>why climate change is happening</u>.

9. When he arrives, I will tell him <u>when we are leaving.</u>

12b. In these sentences, identify the nominal clauses and then identify their functions in each sentence. The clauses can be direct objects, subjects, indirect objects, object complements, predicate nominatives, or other functions. Watch out for other uses of *that*, including the relative pronoun.

1. The statement summarizes what he is saying.

2. We will learn if tickets are still available.

3. When we will meet again is the next topic.

4. I have a question about who broke the equipment.

5. I will tell whoever is interested about the news.

6. I don't know why he left.

7. His claim was that he was abducted by aliens.

8. His wife made him what he is today.

9. I don't think that we should blame that on his wife.

10. We were taught that anything that is worth doing is worth doing well.

13 They're *So* Dependent

Distinguishing Dependent Clauses

We've learned that there are three kinds of **dependent clauses**: subordinate clauses, relative clauses, and nominal clauses.

Sometimes nominal clauses superficially resemble subordinate or relative clauses. This chapter will help you get better at recognizing each kind.

First, let's review.

Subordinate clauses are adverbial. They can modify verbs, adjectives, and other adverbs. When modifying verbs, they are usually moveable. They always begin with a subordinating conjunction:

While I have been working, the phone has been ringing.
The phone has been ringing **while** I have been working.

Since my assistant left, my job has been harder.
My job has been harder **since** my assistant left,

Arthur is **so** generous **that** he never thinks of himself.

She runs faster **than** anyone I've ever seen.

Relative clauses are adjectival, following nouns and occasionally pronouns. They begin with relative pronouns or relative adverbs and follow the nouns they modify.

Ed is the man **who** told me that story.
The report **that** shocked me is summarized in the papers.
It was he **who** called you earlier.
We ate at the restaurant in Portland **where** we first met.

Nominal clauses can fill noun positions just about anywhere in a sentence. Nominalizers or question words appear at the beginning of nominal clauses:

I wonder **if** he will come to the party.
I think **that** he will come.
I wondered **why** you left early.
We have learned **how** the mistake was made.
Whoever speaks up will be heard.
She can see **whomever** she likes.

DISTINGUISHING NOMINAL CLAUSES FROM SUBORDINATE CLAUSES

As we saw in the last chapter, nominal clauses are introduced by question words (*who, what, where, when, why, how,* and others) or by nominalizers (*that, if,* or *whether*):

I know **when** they arrive.
I know **where** they will arrive.
I'll decide **whether** we will go.
I wonder **if** the weather will be pleasant.

You can often recognize nominal clauses because they fill noun positions in their sentences: subjects, direct objects, predicate nominatives, appositives, and others. In most sentences that contain nominal clauses, you can replace each nominal with a noun without changing the grammar of the rest of the sentence:

I know **Bob.**
I know **Milwaukee.**
I'll decide **the matter.**

An exception is the word *wonder*:

I wonder **if** the weather will be pleasant.

Wonder can be a transitive verb with a direct object *only* if the direct object is a nominal clause.
Here are some more examples:

My question is **what** happened to Ralph? [a predicate nominative]
What happened to Ralph is the question. [a subject]
I have learned **what** happened to Ralph. [a direct object]

Subordinate clauses, which are adverbial, may superficially resemble nominal clauses because some subordinating conjunctions look like question words and nominalizers:

I always meet them **when** they arrive.
I'll meet them **whether or not** they are on time.
I'll meet them **if** they are on time.

But it's usually easy to distinguish subordinates from nominals. The subordinates—because they are adverbial—are often moveable; they can be shifted to the beginning or end of the sentence:

When they arrive, I always meet them.
Whether or not they are on time, I'll meet them.
If they are on time, I'll meet them.

Nominal clauses can never be shifted this way.
Before we go further, let's practice distinguishing these clauses.

EXERCISES:
Distinguish Nominals from Subordinates

13a. In the following sentences, classify the underlined dependent clauses as either subordinate or nominal.

1. I will see <u>if we have any milk</u>.

2. I will go to the store <u>if we are out of milk</u>.

3. <u>Whether or not we are out of milk</u>, I will go to the store.

4. I wonder <u>whether we are out of milk</u>.

5. I go to the store <u>when we are out of milk</u>.

6. I will know <u>whether we are out of milk</u>.

7. I can't understand <u>how we could be out of milk</u>.

8. I don't know <u>why we are out of milk</u>.

9. <u>Why we are out of milk</u> is <u>what I want to know</u>.

10. I told you <u>that we would run out of milk</u>.

13b. In this next set, identify the dependent clauses and classify them as either subordinate or nominal.

1. Go see if Jim is here.

2. We will start dinner if Jim is here.

3. If Jim is here, we can have dinner.

4. If Jim is here is what I want to know.

5. I need to know whether Jim has arrived.

6. Whether or not he has arrived, we will now have dinner.

7. When Jim arrives, we will have dinner.

8. I know when Jim will arrive.

9. Please tell me how we can have dinner if Jim is not here.

Distinguishing Nominal Clauses from Relative Clauses

Relative clauses and nominal clauses may also resemble each other superficially.

Relative clauses are adjectival. They follow the nouns they modify, and they are introduced by relative pronouns (*who, whom, whose, that, which*) or by relative adverbs (*where, when*):

There's the book **that** I need.
This is the place **where** I lost my keys.

In both cases, the relative pronoun or adverb has a grammatical role in its relative clause. The pronouns, of course, have noun functions, and the relative adverbs have adverb functions.

Here are two small points that are sometimes helpful:

1. In relative clauses introduced by the relative pronoun *that*, the pronoun can usually be replaced by *which* without a significant change in meaning:

There's the book **that** I need.
There's the book **which** I need.

There's the cat **that** scratched me.
There's the cat **which** scratched me.

2. In relative clauses introduced by the relative pronoun *who*, the pronoun can usually be replaced by *that* without a change in meaning:

There's the man **who** helped me.
There's the man **that** helped me.

There's the woman **whom** I need to see.
There's the woman **that** I need to see.

Nominal clauses may superficially resemble relative clauses because they sometimes begin with question words that are identical to relative pronouns (*who, whom, whose,* or *which*), or identical to the relative adverbs *when* and *where*.

Nominal clauses may also begin with the nominalizer *that*, which is identical to the relative pronoun *that*.

In distinguishing relative clauses from nominal clauses, remember these differences:

1. In relative clauses, the relative pronoun always plays a grammatical role in its clause, and the relative clause always follows the noun it modifies.

2. Nominal clauses will fill a noun position in the sentence; they do *not* always follow a noun, though they sometimes do.

Also, in the *that-if-whether* clauses, the nominalizer plays no role at all in its clause, so the nominalizer *that* absolutely cannot be replaced by *which*:

RIGHT: I know **that** the weather will be pleasant.
IMPOSSIBLE: I know **which** the weather will be pleasant.

RIGHT: I am sure **that** we have met before.
IMPOSSIBLE: I am sure **which** we have met before.

With these points in mind, let's work with some sentences.

EXERCISES:

Distinguish Nominals from Relatives

13c. Classify the underlined dependent clauses as either *relative* (adjectival) clauses or as *nominal* clauses:

1. I know that she likes me.

2. That she likes me surprises me.

3. That is the class that I want.

4. That is the class that challenges me.

5. The people who like me are over there.

6. I know who likes you.

7. What fascinates me is calculus.

8. We'll learn why spring begins.

9. The day when spring begins is next week.

10. I know the place where I can enroll.

13d. Identify the dependent clauses in these sentences and classify them as *relative* (adjectival) clauses or *nominal* clauses:

1. I know who that is.

2. I will take the book that is least expensive.

3. There is the fellow whom I've met before.

4. I know whom you spoke with.

5. There is the woman who hired me.

6. The dog that bit me is in that yard.

7. Who steals my purse steals my gum.

8. I have learned what the answer is.

Distinguishing Subordinate Clauses from Relative Clauses

Once again, subordinate clauses are adverbial, but they may superficially resemble relative clauses because some subordinating conjunctions (*that; so . . . that; when;* or *where*) look like the relative pronoun *that* or the relative adverbs *when* and *where*.

We'll remind you again about these differences:

1. Subordinate clauses, being adverbial, are usually moveable when they modify verbs, but relative clauses are never moveable.

2. Subordinate clauses modify verbs and, less often, adjectives or adverbs. Relative clauses modify nouns and pronouns.

3. Subordinate clauses begin with subordinating conjunctions, while relative clauses begin with relative pronouns or relative adverbs.

Here are some examples of subordinate clauses, using conjunctions that might be mistaken for relative pronouns or relative adverbs:

I begin my garden **when** spring begins.
(**When** spring begins, I begin my garden.)

There is hope **where** there is life.
(**Where** there is life, there is hope.)

My mother is happy **that** I have chosen my major.
(This subordinate clause, modifying *happy*, is not moveable.)

Here are examples of relative clauses. The first two use the relative adverbs, and the third uses the relative pronoun *that*.

Spring is the season **when** I begin gardening.
There is the place **where** I always have my garden.
My neighbors enjoy the vegetables **that** I raise in my garden.

EXERCISES

Distinguish Subordinates from Relatives

13e. This time identify the dependent clauses in the following sentences and classify them as *relative* or as *subordinate*. Some sentences have two dependent clauses:

1. Because it is late, tomorrow we will see the movie that you want to see.

2. When we saw *The Martian*, we enjoyed the story about the space traveler who is marooned alone on a planet.

3. We were quite surprised by the film that we saw last night.

4. This is the theatre where we saw that film.

5. Is this the time when the next film is shown?

6. You should tell your friends when you see a good film.

7. Where I come from, we have several good movie theatres.

13f. Finally, here's an exercise that brings together all the concepts in this chapter. Identify the dependent clauses in the following sentences and classify them as *relative*, as *subordinate*, or as *nominal* clauses:

1. The place that we call home is Peoria.

2. I must see if they are here.

3. I know that they have arrived.

4. I read an article about the accident that we saw yesterday.

5. We will see if the storm will hit.

6. If the storm hits, we will be ready.

7. I know the time when they will arrive.

8. The town where I was born is very small.

9. I wonder where he was born.

10. I will go to the airport when he arrives.

11. Whether we want to go or not, we must be at the airport.

12. I do not know whether he will be on the plane.

What, More?

Verbs and Voice, Infinitives, and Passive Complements

Verbs, we've said, are regarded as the most important part of English sentences because they contain so much information. That information is reflected in the many forms verbs can take. Here, we examine more of those forms and the changes they cause in other parts of the sentence.

VERBS HAVE VOICE: ACTIVE AND PASSIVE

In Chapter 8 on complements, we discussed two classes of action verbs called **transitive** and **intransitive**:

    INTRANSITIVE: He sang.
    TRANSITIVE: He sang a song.

    INTRANSITIVE: She wrote.
    TRANSITIVE: She wrote a novel.

We said that verbs are transitive when they have direct objects, as in the examples above. Linking verbs are never transitive.

Now we learn another thing: Transitive verbs—and only transitives—are capable of two **voices**: active and passive.

With **active voice verbs**, the subject is the performer of the action and the direct object is the receiver of the action.

The batter hit the ball.

In **passive voice verbs**, the subject is the receiver of the action. The performer is deleted from the sentence, or it is shifted to the end of the sentence in a prepositional phrase:

The ball was hit.
The ball was hit by the batter.

In passive verbs, the main verb is always a **past participle** and the auxiliary just before the main verb is a form of *be*:

You were made chairman by the club.
She has been elected chairwoman.
She is known to everyone in the club.

REVISING PASSIVES INTO ACTIVES

It's often helpful to rewrite passive sentences as active sentences. It's easy to rewrite this passive sentence:

You were made chairman by the club.

Simply shift *the club* to the subject position and *you* to the direct object position. In this case, *chairman* becomes an object complement.

The club made you chairman.

But what do we do when the sentence contains no performer of the action?

She has been elected chairwoman.

In cases like this, we must either locate a performer in the larger context, or leave the passive unchanged. Here are some more passive sentences, and their active voice counterparts:

PASSIVE: The news was heard by me on the radio.
ACTIVE: I heard the news on the radio.

PASSIVE: The essay was graded by the teacher.
ACTIVE: The teacher graded the essay.

PASSIVE: The room was refurnished by our landlord.
ACTIVE: Our landlord refurnished the room.

THE PASSIVE COMPLEMENTS

Previously, we've discussed **complements** in active sentences. In particular, we've discussed transitive verbs and direct objects, indirect objects, and object complements.

Some passive verbs take complements, too, called **passive complements**. Let's begin with this active voice sentence:

1. Dad gave **Mom** her present.

Here *Mom* is the indirect object; *her present* is the direct object.

We can rewrite Sentence 1 in the passive voice like this:

2. **Mom** was given her present by Dad.

In Sentence 2, *Mom* is now the subject. We've made the subject in Sentence 1, *Dad*, the object of a preposition. And *her present* remains the direct object in Sentence 2. This can only be done with active sentences that contain an indirect object as well as a direct object.

Here are more pairs of sentences—the first active and the second passive—with <u>direct objects underlined</u> and indirect objects in **bold**:

ACTIVE: Ed brought **Ralph** <u>some hot soup</u>.
PASSIVE: Ralph was brought <u>some hot soup</u> by Ed.

ACTIVE: Dad showed **Jimmy** <u>the door</u>.
PASSIVE: Jimmy was shown <u>the door</u> by Dad.

ACTIVE: Mr. Redden read **the class** <u>a poem</u>.
PASSIVE: The class was read <u>a poem</u> by Mr. Redden.

When the direct object in an active sentence remains the direct object in the passive version of the same sentence, the object in the passive sentence is sometimes called a *retained object*. But we'll simply call it the direct object.

Some sentences with object complements can also be made passive:

1. The club elected **Ralph** <u>sixth vice-president</u>.

Here *Ralph* is the direct object and *sixth vice-president* is the object complement. When we make the sentence passive, *Ralph* becomes the subject:

2. Ralph was elected <u>sixth vice-president</u> by the club.

In Sentence 2, the object complement of Sentence 1, *sixth vice-president*, is now a predicate nominative.

In the following examples, we will see object complements (underlined in the active sentences) become predicate nominatives or predicate adjectives in the passive sentences. The direct objects are in bold:

ACTIVE: We made **Mom** <u>angry</u>.
PASSIVE: Mom was made <u>angry</u> by us. (Predicate adjective)

ACTIVE: The chairman appointed **Bob** <u>secretary</u>.
PASSIVE: Bob was appointed <u>secretary</u> by the chairman. (Predicate nominative)

ACTIVE: The class declared **Ruthie** <u>the winner</u>.
PASSIVE: Ruthie was declared <u>the winner</u> by the class. (Predicate nominative)

As you may have noticed, all of the passive sentences you read are awkward and wordy. Active versions are often shorter and more direct than passives. Some of the passives might also be improved by simply deleting the prepositional phrases, as in *Bob was appointed secretary*.

INFINITIVE VERBS

All verbs (except some of the auxiliary verbs) have an important form that we have not yet discussed: the **infinitive** form. In English, an infinitive verb is simply the first-person present tense of the verb (like *buy, sell, cook, bake, talk, walk*) preceded by the word *to*. In this context, *to* is called a particle and is simply part of the infinitive. All of these are infinitive verbs:

to buy	to sell	to hyperventilate
to bake	to talk	to negotiate
to inflate	to cook	

All of these sentences contain infinitive verbs:

My son is learning <u>to speak</u> French.
She wants <u>to take</u> a course <u>to learn</u> <u>to speak</u> well in public.
We need <u>to meet</u> <u>to discuss</u> the contracts.

As you can see, infinitive verbs are important structures that we use every day. We'll discuss their uses in another chapter soon.

For now, notice the difference between infinitive verbs and prepositional phrases beginning with *to*. In prepositional phrases, *to* is typically followed by a noun or pronoun, not a verb. These are prepositional phrases:

We're going to Oregon this summer.
I'll mail postcards to my friends.

And these are infinitives, with verbs—not nouns or pronouns—after *to*:

We're going to travel this summer.
I'm ready to mail our cards.

PHRASAL VERBS

Phrasal verbs are two-word verbs used as one word. The second word, called a **particle**, always looks like a preposition but without an object:

I'll look up the word.
I'll write out a check.
We'll wait out the storm.
She looked in on the kids
We signed up for a class.
They took off an hour ago.
He sat in on the meeting.
We have put up with this long enough.

Although the particle looks like a preposition, it cannot be the beginning of a prepositional phrase. Notice the differences:

I'll look up the word. (A phrasal verb)
I'll look up the chimney. (A prepositional phrase.)

Despite disappointment, they <u>went on</u>. (A phrasal verb)
They went <u>on the train</u>. (A prepositional phrase.)

In some phrasal verbs, other words (especially direct objects) can appear between the main verb and the particle:

I'll <u>look</u> the word <u>up</u>.
I'll <u>write</u> the check <u>out</u>.
He <u>built</u> his confidence <u>up</u>.
I'll <u>check</u> the information <u>out</u>.

There is another verbal pattern that may resemble a phrasal verb. Consider these sentences:

I've <u>put up</u> with you long enough.
I'll <u>put</u> the book <u>up</u> on the shelf.

In the first, *put up* is a phrasal verb. In the second, *put* is the verb and *up* is neither a particle nor a preposition, but simply an adverb. (Compare *I'll put the book down* or *I'll put the book aside*.)

Don't confuse the term *phrasal verbs* with the similar term *verb phrase*.

POINTS FOR WRITERS

1. When to use active and passive verbs.

Active voice sentences are often more effective than passive voice sentences. The active voice is usually more concise and direct. Compare these two sentences:

Chris <u>is reading</u> *The Lord of the Rings* for the second time.

The Lord of the Rings <u>is being read</u> by Chris for the second time.

In the first sentence, the subject is actively performing the action. The sentence is clearly about *Chris*, not the book, so it's a reasonable choice to make *Chris* the subject.

But there are times when we do want to focus on the recipient of the action, as in this passive sentence, which we might see in our newspapers or hear in a broadcast:

A convenience store on Fifth Street was robbed last night.

If the writer does not yet know who performed this action, the passive may well be the better choice here. (Of course, we might also write *Someone robbed a convenience store. . . .*)

Consider this example:

John F. Kennedy was elected President in 1960.

We all *know* that American voters, or a substantial number of them, elected Kennedy, and the writer may be intending to focus on Kennedy, not the electorate. The passive voice makes sense here.

Although the passive certainly has its uses, prefer the active voice unless you have a good reason for the passive.

EXERCISES

14a. Rewrite the following passive voice sentences as active voice sentences, as in this example:

PASSIVE: I was given a prescription by my doctor.
ACTIVE: My doctor gave me a prescription.

1. Your letter was received by me.

2. I was made happy by your letter.

3. I was given instructions today by my supervisor.

4. My last essay was given a C by my English teacher.

5. I was seen at the mall by Cheryl.

6. The mail was delivered by the postman at noon.

7. After the symphony was played beautifully by the orchestra, the composer was praised by the critics.

14b. In the passive sentences above, locate, underline, and identify the passive complements: the direct object (DO), the predicate adjective (PA), and the predicate nominate (PN), as in this example:

DO
PASSIVE: I was given <u>a prescription</u> by my doctor last night.

14c. Distinguish phrasal verbs from verbs followed by prepositional phrases, as in these examples:

I'll <u>turn on</u> the television.
[Phrasal verb]

That new car can turn <u>on a dime</u>.
[Verb with prepositional phrase]

1. We'll turn off the highway at the next exit.
   Please turn off the radio.

2. The news comes on at 10 pm.
    The gifts came on Christmas Eve.

3. The pumpkin turned into a beautiful coach.
    We'll turn into this driveway.

4. We will now take up the collection.
    They took the dresser up the stairs.

5. He called out to her before she drove away.
    He called out the window.

15 They're *So* Common

More on Nouns

We've not yet dealt with important features of nouns and associated functions and structures, including some you may already know. Here we discuss several of them.

THE COMMON AND THE PROPER

You may already know about common and proper nouns. **Common nouns** are words like *man, woman, child, city, state*. They name general, nonspecific persons or things. **Proper nouns** name particular persons or things, and they're capitalized: *Henry, Annie, Herbert, St. Louis, Missouri*. (There are no *improper* nouns, and if there are, being very proper ourselves, we refuse to discuss them.)

Usually, it's easy to know when to capitalize a noun, but there can be uncertainty about words that may—or may not—be official titles:

I spoke with Doctor Smith yesterday.
I spoke with the doctor of obstetrics yesterday.

The president of the club lives in that white house.
The President lives in the White House.

Context often has a great deal to do with this. (When Dr. Smith has his business cards printed, the words *Doctor of Obstetrics* are capitalized.) To make these decisions, notice what is being done in contexts similar to yours.

Dictionaries can help us make these distinctions, but it's also helpful to notice what other writers do in similar situations.

PLURAL NOUNS

As you know, we make most nouns plural by simply adding *–s* to the end.

If a word ends with *s, x, z, sh,* or *ch*, we add *–es*: *basses, boxes, dishes, churches,* and many others.

But there are quite a few exceptions—called **irregular plurals**—and for these, all of us may need to refer to a dictionary at times. The easiest irregular plurals are those that don't change from singular to plural: *Sheep, deer,* and *moose* don't change.

Still other familiar irregulars change a vowel within the word (*mice, men, teeth,* and more) or add *–en*: *oxen, children*.

With a noun that ends with a consonant and *o*, we usually use *–es* for the plural: *heroes, zeroes, potatoes*.

But there are other nouns that end with a consonant and *o* that take only *-s*. Some of these are musical terms from Italian: *pianos, cellos, solos*.

A noun that ends with a vowel followed by *o* also takes only *–s* for the plural: *patios, radios, rodeos, zoos*.

With some nouns that end with *f* or *fe*, follow the familiar rule: Change the *f* to *v* and add *–es*: *calves, halves, knives, wives*. But other plurals that end with *f* or *fe* take only *–s*: *roofs, proofs, handkerchiefs, beliefs*.

You probably recall that in nouns that end with a consonant and *y*, we change *y* to *i* and add *–es*: *armies, ladies, rallies*. But when a vowel precedes *y*, we add only *–s*: *bays, boys, alleys, valleys*.

And then there are a number of words from Latin or Greek that retain their original plural forms or something similar. To us, these plurals seem quite irregular:

alumnae	phenomena
alumni	radii
criteria	stimuli
media	theses
nebulae	vertebrae

We'll remind you again that a dictionary always helps with words like these. Most writers will use few of these Latin and Greek plurals, but we all need to remember some, including (probably) these:

- *medium* (the singular) and *media*, as in *the medium of television*
- *criterion* and *criteria*
- *phenomenon* and *phenomena*
- *crisis* and *crises*

Almost every profession and academic subject has its special terms that include certain irregular plurals, and it's a good idea to learn them as soon as possible for your professional writing.

It's also helpful to know that almost no one uses *memorandum* and *memoranda* anymore; we simply write *memo* or *memos*. And for most purposes today, *data* is accepted as both singular and plural.

GREAT INDECISIONS: POSSESSION AND APOSTROPHES

It's usually easy to indicate possession in English nouns; with singular nouns, we add an apostrophe and *–s*: *man's, woman's, child's, Oliver's, Stanley's*.

With plurals, we add a lone apostrophe after the final –s: *friends', students', teachers'*.

But the English language sometimes makes things a bit trickier. When a plural does not end in –s, we make the possessive form with the apostrophe first, then –s, like the regular singular possessive: *men's, women's, children's*.

Now comes the frustrating part: Suppose a singular noun ends in –s, like *boss* or *Ross, Charles* or *Bess*? For the possessive, do we add only an apostrophe? (*Ross', Charles',* or *Bess'* ?) Or do we add an apostrophe and –s? (*Ross's, Charles's,* or *Bess's*?)

The sad truth is that American English has no universally accepted way of marking possession in these cases. Some authorities insist on one way, some on another.

In your professional writing, you must find out which way your organization prefers and stick to it. If your organization has no standard way, persuade your leaders to adopt one of the standard style guides (like the *Associated Press Stylebook*) to answer such questions.

In this book, we create possessives with –'s after singulars ending in *s*, like this:

The boss's desk
Ross's desk
Bess's desk

APPOSITIVES

An **appositive** is a noun or pronoun that usually appears immediately after another noun to rename the first noun and provide additional information about it. The appositive is usually enclosed in a pair of commas, although we may sometimes use dashes or parentheses depending on our desired style, tone, or emphasis.

More than one appositive is possible, and sometimes the appositive has modifiers of its own:

My boss, <u>Mr. Smith,</u> was talking to my parents.

Mr. Smith, <u>my wonderful boss</u>, was talking to my parents.

My boss—<u>that bore, that ogre, that man whom I hate more than any other person living, with the possible exception of my English teacher</u>—was telling my parents that I have a bad attitude.

In the sentences above, the appositives all rename the subject (*My boss* or *Mr. Smith*), and for that reason they are considered part of the subject.

In the third example, the dashes are helpful to mark the beginning and end of the long, complicated appositive phrase because the phrase itself contains three commas.

Nominal clauses can be appositives:

The physicist's idea, **that** <u>multiple universes exist</u>, baffles me.

My question—**who** <u>killed Colonel Mustard in the library?</u>—remains unanswered.

His topic, **why** <u>climate change is happening</u>, was timely.

When pronouns are used as appositives, their case (nominative, objective, or possessive) should match the function of the nouns they rename. In the example below, the appositives rename the object (*judges*) of a preposition, so the pronoun is in the objective case:

The photos were given to the judges, <u>Eric and **me**</u>.

In the next example, the appositives rename the subject (*judges*), so the pronoun is in the nominative case:

The judges, <u>Eric and **I**,</u> will study the photos.

Sometimes structures look like appositives but are not. For instance, a compound noun phrase, joined with *or*, can be used to indicate a synonym:

The common dog, <u>or *Canis lupus familiaris*</u>, belongs to the Canidae family.

Mergenthaler's typesetting machine (<u>or *Linotype*</u>) was completed in 1884.

The noun after *or* is not an appositive, despite the punctuation. But remove the conjunction *or* and the same sentences now contain appositives that are, again, synonyms of the preceding noun phrase:

The common dog, <u>*Canis lupus familiaris*</u>, belongs to the Canidae family.

Mergenthaler's typesetting machine, <u>the *Linotype*</u>, was completed in 1884.

Don't confuse the appositive with adjectives that appear after the noun they modify:

The children, <u>noisy and enthusiastic</u>, dashed through the living room.

THE EXPLETIVE *THERE*

An **expletive**, as the term is used in grammar, is a word inserted into a sentence that adds nothing to the meaning but alters word order in ways that are sometimes useful. As we use the term here, expletives are *not* swear words, although the term sometimes has that meaning, too: "Where are my [expletive deleted] glasses?"

The most commonly used expletive is *there*, which can be added to a sentence to temporarily take the place of the subject.

This expletive postpones the appearance of the subject, which may be a noun or a pronoun, until after the first word of the verb (that is, after the first auxiliary or after the main verb when there is no auxiliary). The expletive is never the actual subject.

Compare these pairs of sentences, in which the complete subject is underlined:

<u>A painting by Degas</u> is hanging in the museum.
There is <u>a painting by Degas</u> hanging in the museum.

<u>Two men</u> were looking for you.
There were <u>two men</u> looking for you.

The expletive *there* has no grammatical function in the second sentence. It has only a stylistic function, to stand in for the true subject, postponing the subject until later in the sentence, as shown above.

In English, expletive constructions are the usual way to say certain things:

There will now be <u>a short intermission</u>.

We don't say, *A short intermission will now be* (though we can say *We'll now have a short intermission.*)

Somewhere **there** is <u>a place for us</u>.

We can't say, *Somewhere a place for us is* or *A place for us is somewhere.*

In both of the cases above, the expletive *there* postpones the subject to the end of the sentence, where the subject (*a short intermission; a place for us*) receives special emphasis.

Don't confuse the expletive *there* with the adverb of place *there*. Here's a useful test: Can you replace *there* with *here* and retain the original general sense of the sentence? If yes, then *there* is an adverb.

ADVERB: Your keys are over there.
(Compare: *Your keys are over here.*)

ADVERB: There are your keys.
(Compare: *Here are your keys.*)

EXPLETIVE: **There** are keys all over the place.
(We wouldn't usually say, *Here are keys all over the place.*)

Here are a few more examples of subjects postponed by the expletive *there*:

A dog is growling in the yard.
There is a dog growling in the yard.

A boy is building something on our porch.
There is a boy building something on the porch.

In Chapter 20, we'll learn about the use of *it* as an expletive.

NOUNS OF DIRECT ADDRESS

In written dialogue and letters, as in daily conversation, we sometimes use the names of the people we're addressing. These names are called **nouns of direct address**:

<u>Mr. Smith</u>, I'd like to speak with you, please.
I don't like to be disappointed, and you, <u>Renfru</u>, disappoint me.

Sometimes nouns of direct address are common nouns that apply to one person or an entire audience:

<u>My friend</u>, I hope you will take my advice.

This news, <u>my friends</u>, should comfort us all.

<u>Ladies and gentlemen</u>, welcome to our forty-first annual vase juggling competition.

The noun of direct address is always enclosed by a pair of commas, and it has no *grammatical* function in the sentence. That is, it's not considered part of the subject or the predicate. It has a *social* function: to get the attention of the person addressed, or to clarify who is being addressed.

Sometimes, if the context doesn't resolve ambiguities, readers may confuse nouns of address and appositives:

Your supervisor, <u>Mr. Watley</u>, told you to finish that project.

If Mr. Watley is the supervisor, then the words *Mr. Watley* are an appositive. If Mr. Watley is the person being addressed, then *Mr. Watley* is a noun of direct address. We can usually depend on the larger context to clarify this.

POINTS FOR WRITERS

1. Restrictive and non-restrictive appositives.

Here comes a distinction that is seldom understood and often ignored.

Sometimes the pair of commas is not used with the appositive, depending on the larger context. In the first example below, the writer has more than one daughter; in the second, he has only one:

My daughter <u>Mary</u> plays the tuba.
My daughter, <u>Mary</u>, plays the tuba.

In the first example, *Mary* is a **restrictive appositive**: it restricts (or limits) the meaning of *daughter*. In the second example, the non-restrictive appositive *Mary* simply provides supplementary information. (And in this case the commas contribute nothing to understanding the sentence.)

Here are more examples of restrictive appositives, followed by **non-restrictive** examples:

RESTRICTIVE: My cousin <u>Bob</u> plays the harmonica.
NON-RESTRICTIVE: My cousin, <u>Bob</u>, plays the harmonica.

RESTRICTIVE: Our custodian <u>Mr. Halley</u> does good work.
NON-RESTRICTIVE: Our custodian, <u>Mr. Halley</u>, does good work.

In both cases the restrictive appositive, without the commas, is used to identify a specific cousin or custodian out of many.

When in doubt, add the commas. Few (if any) readers will object, or even notice, if you're wrong, and the commas seldom if ever alter the meaning of the sentence significantly. But if you add the first comma, don't forget the second.

EXERCISES

15a. What's the difference <u>in writing</u> between regular plural nouns, possessive nouns, and plural possessive nouns? Write an example that illustrates each category, using words that have regular plurals.

For example: *cats, cat's,* and *cats'.*

15b. Write plural, singular possessive, and plural possessive forms of the following nouns: *woman, ox, church, tomato, piano, medium* (e.g., *the medium of TV*), *boss,* and *octopus.* Use a dictionary when you need to.

15c. In the following sentences, identify the sentences that contain nouns of address, appositives, and expletives, and underline those structures. In sentences with expletives, identify the complete subject of the sentence. A sentence may contain more than one of these structures. In some cases, the function of the phrase may not be clear within the limited context.

Examples:

> My brother <u>Ed</u> has left. [Appositive]
> <u>Dwight</u>, see if his brother has left. [Noun of address]
> There are <u>no printer cartridges</u> in the supply closet.
> [*There* is an expletive, and *no printer cartridges* is the subject.]

1. Dr. Kildare, you can speak with my assistant.

2. June, speak with my physician, Dr. Kildare.

3. Your brother, Alice, is remarkable.

4. There is rain forecast for tomorrow.

5. It is clear that Ed is a menace.

16

Zowie!

Interjections and the Eight Parts of Speech

The **interjection** is a common grammatical category, and a simple one, for any word or group of words that we use to express shock, surprise, pain, joy, admiration, and a wide range of other feelings and responses.

INTERJECTIONS

Interjections are used by themselves or as part of a sentence:

Good grief!
Cool!
Oh, no!
My.
What now?

Interjections have no distinctive form. They can be single words or longer phrases; they can be joined to sentences by commas or dashes, or they can stand independently, ending with periods, question marks, or exclamation marks:

What the heck?
Well, *great*.

Wow!
Oy!

Some interjections serve social purposes: greetings (*Hello, Goodbye*); pauses (*Let's see, Well . . .*); politeness (*Please, Thanks*); or agreement or disagreement (*Yes, No, Yeah, Nah, Maybe, Sure! Says you! Yeah, right! Baloney!*).

Some interjections are the kinds of words you use when you drop a hammer on your foot—the words your mother told you to stop using. (You *know* the words we mean.)

Other interjections are not even actual words, but merely sounds that have become conventional ways to express things: *Ouch! Yikes! Sheesh! Oof! Oops! Hubba-hubba! Whoopee!* and, in the upper Midwestern states, *Uff-da!* They are generally easy to recognize.

The most important thing to know about interjections is that, although they are useful for self-expression and social interaction, they play no grammatical role in the sentence. In analyzing the grammar of a sentence, you can disregard the interjections.

Some grammar books classify some of these words as adverbs, though they clearly do not modify verbs, adjectives, or other adverbs. (Some could arguably be sentence modifiers, which we'll examine in Chapter 20.) For our purposes, calling them interjections is sufficient.

THE EIGHT PARTS OF SPEECH

The eight **parts of speech** belong to that body of general knowledge all educated people are supposed to possess—like the three branches of government, the Four Horsemen of the Apocalypse, the five Marx Brothers, the six basic nutrients, the Seven Deadly Sins, and all nine of the eight planets.

In other words, they're an essential idea in the study of language. The eight parts of speech are eight categories used in conventional grammar study to account for all the words in English. Every word in English can be placed into one of these categories—or at least one—and we've now learned a good deal about all the categories.

Three of the parts of speech are nouns or words associated with nouns:

Nouns: Words that stand for persons, places, things, or ideas.
Pronouns: Words that take the place of nouns.
Adjectives: Words that modify nouns or pronouns.

Two of the parts of speech are verbs and adverbs:

Verbs: Words that indicate an action or a state of being.
Adverbs: Words that modify verbs, adjectives, or other adverbs.

Two of the parts of speech are connecting words:

Conjunctions: Words that connect phrases and clauses to other phrases or clauses; they indicate some grammatical relationship between the connected units.
Prepositions: Words that connect a noun or pronoun (the object of the preposition) with other words in the sentence to create adjectival or adverbial phrases.

And the eighth part of speech are the **interjections,** which we've just met. Interjections, again, are exclamatory words and phrases used to express feelings and reactions.

An important part of analyzing the grammar of any sentence is to place each word into one of the eight parts. That's not always easy. To be honest, a few words just don't fit well into any of these eight categories. The expletive *there* is one.

A FORM AND ITS FUNCTIONS

In analyzing the grammar of a sentence, it's helpful to distinguish between a **form** and its **functions**:

The **form** can be any word, like a noun or a verb. It can also be a larger unit constructed upon a part of speech, like a verb phrase or a prepositional phrase.

The **function** is the grammatical role the form plays in a particular sentence. A noun can function as a subject or direct object. Or, as we've seen, nouns can have other functions: They can be indirect objects, predicate nominatives, objects of a preposition, or other functions. Similarly, prepositional phrases can be adjectival or adverbial.

A number of forms (nouns, verbs, modifiers) assembled together can build larger phrases and clauses that have their own functions. A relative clause is a form that has an adjectival function in a sentence; a subordinate clause has an adverbial function.

The function of any form is defined by the way it is used in a particular sentence, that is, by its context. You can't look at a single word in isolation and define its function. There are exceptions: It's usually safe to say that *the* is an article, used adjectivally. But in the sentence that you just read, *the* was used as a noun, as the subject of a clause: "*The* is an article."

Consider this word: *bill*. Is it a noun or a verb? To answer, we need context:

I will bring your monthly <u>bills</u>.
He will <u>bill</u> me every month.

In the first sentence, *bill* is a noun, and it functions as a direct object. In the second sentence, *bill* is a transitive verb; it functions as the main verb of the sentence.

Or consider these sentences:

I am <u>rising</u> early tomorrow morning.
I like <u>rising</u> early.
I like to watch the <u>rising</u> sun.

In the first sentence, *rising* has the form of a verb (because of its *–ing* suffix), and it also has the function of a verb, as part of a progressive tense verb, *am rising*.

In the second sentence, *rising* again has the form a verb, the present participle of *rise*, but it has the function of a noun, the direct object of the transitive verb *like*. (What does the speaker like? He likes *rising* early.)

In the third sentence, *rising* still has the form of a verb, but it has the function of an adjective, modifying *sun*. (We'll soon learn more about using verbs nominally and adjectivally.)

There are other challenges in classification: For instance, how do we classify particles? You'll recall that a **particle**, as we have used the term, is the first element in an infinitive verb (as in <u>to</u> look or <u>to</u> do: *I need time <u>to look</u> at my list of things <u>to do</u>*) or the second element in a phrasal verb (*<u>look up</u> a word*). We simply consider these particles as parts of their verbs; they are not regarded as separate words.

And the expletive *there*, since it doesn't participate in the grammatical structure of a sentence, doesn't fit neatly into any grammatical category.

Although we have not discussed the distinction between form and function before, we've used the distinction here and there in this book. Early on, we said that nouns could be used adverbially, and that some adverbs could be used nominally. Form and function are important ideas in grammar.

We'll see that this matter of form and function becomes particularly important as we move on to chapters about verbals.

EXERCISES

16a. Write from memory the Eight Parts of Speech. Then define them and check your work by referring to the early pages of this chapter.

16b. In the following sentences, use context to identify both the form and function of the underlined words.

1. In the increasingly chaotic country, university students are <u>revolting</u>.

2. Defend them if you like, but I'm tired of these <u>revolting</u> students.

3. We were <u>jogging</u> around the block.

4. All of us enjoy <u>jogging</u>.

5. He will replace the <u>shattered</u> lamp.

6. He <u>shattered</u> it accidentally.

7. This rose bud is <u>for</u> you.

8. I gave you a rose bud, <u>for</u> I care about you.

9. I wanted to get you more, <u>but</u> I couldn't afford it.

10. I bought you nothing <u>but</u> this rose bud.

17 Those Verbing Verbals

Gerunds and Participles

A **verbal** is a verb that doesn't mind its own business. It is a verb in *form* with a different *function*—it's a verb behaving like another part of speech. (The nerve of some verbs.) A verbal can function as a noun, an adjective, or an adverb.

While verbals are used as other parts of speech, they retain some of the important qualities of verbs. For example, they can take direct objects and indirect objects and other complements, and they can be modified by adverbs. Because they're versatile, verbals are enormously useful to writers who understand the power of verbs and want to work as much action into their sentences as possible.

There are only three kinds of verbals, and in this chapter we'll discuss the two simplest kinds: **gerunds** and **participles**. The **infinitives** will come next.

GERUNDS: VERBS AS NOUNS

A **gerund** appears only in the present participle form (the *–ing* form) and it's always used as a noun:

I enjoy baking.
And I enjoy hiking.

And I also enjoy <u>reading</u>.
Once, I tried <u>reading</u> and <u>hiking</u> at the same time, and it did not go well.

In all the sentences above, the gerund phrase (underlined) functions as a direct object. Some gerunds, created from transitive verbs, can also take their own direct objects.

In both of the following sentences, the underlined portion includes the gerund, which is the direct object of the sentences, and another noun phrase, which is the direct object of the verbal:

I enjoy <u>baking **cakes**</u>.
I enjoy <u>reading **books**</u>.

Gerunds can also take indirect objects:

I enjoy <u>baking **my friends** cakes</u>.
I enjoy <u>reading **my son** books</u>.

Notice that these last examples are each, in a way, a combination of two clauses. The second example could be said to contain these two ideas:

I enjoy reading.
I read my child books.

We reduced the second sentence above (*I read my child books*) into a gerund phrase: *I enjoy <u>reading my child books</u>*.

That's why gerund phrases (and verbal phrases of all kinds) are sometimes called *reduced clauses*. They are not true clauses, but the information that they contain could be the basis of a clause.

We can also make gerunds out of transitive verbs with object complements:

We regret <u>making Albert **angry**</u>.

In this sentence, the entire gerund phrase, *making Albert angry*, is the direct object of *regret*. Within the phrase, *Albert* is the direct object of *making*, and *angry* is the object complement describing *Albert*.

Gerunds created from linking verbs can be used with predicate nouns and predicate adjectives. In the next two sentences, the verbal phrase is a direct object of the transitive verb *enjoys*:

Stanley enjoys <u>being a **comedian**</u>.
Oliver enjoys <u>being **funny**</u>.

In both these sentences, the gerund *being* is created from a linking verb. In the first sentence, *comedian* is a predicate nominative; in the second, *funny* is a predicate adjective.

Gerunds can be subjects:

<u>Singing</u> is his favorite pastime.
<u>Becoming a **musician**</u> is his goal.
(The phrase *a musician* is the predicate nominative of *becoming*.)

Below, *singing* has a direct object:

<u>Singing **hymns**</u> is his favorite pastime.

And here, gerund phrases are appositives:

His pastime, <u>singing **hymns**</u>, has made him many friends.

His other pastime, <u>telling naughty **stories**</u>, has lost him a few friends.

A gerund phrase can also be the object of a preposition:

He always has time for <u>singing **hymns**</u>.
He has talked about <u>becoming a **musician**</u>

PARTICIPLES: VERBS AS ADJECTIVES

Now we need to remember two forms of verbs: The present participles of verbs (the *–ing* forms) and the past participles of verbs (the forms used with *have*, as in *have known* or *had seen*).

These forms are used to create adjectival phrases that *precede* the noun. In some sentence structures, with the right punctuation, they can also follow the noun:

The <u>soaring</u> airplane roared overhead.
The airplane, <u>soaring,</u> roared overhead.

<u>Walking quickly to the door</u>, the detective threw it open.
The detective, <u>walking quickly to the door</u>, threw it open.

We watched the snow <u>falling softly</u>.
We watched the <u>softly falling</u> snow.

<u>Shaken from his fall</u>, the old man sat for a moment.
The old man, <u>shaken from his fall</u>, sat for a moment.

<u>Heard across the street</u>, the scream disturbed the neighbors.
The scream, <u>heard across the street</u>, disturbed the neighbors.

As these examples illustrate, the participle can be accompanied by adverbs. And the participle phrase should usually be close to the noun it modifies.

Participles created from transitive verbs can have their own direct objects:

<u>Shoveling **snow**</u>, Mr. Lochenhocher grew tired.

Reading **the poem** aloud, Mrs. Mays grew emotional.
Taking **his time**, Bill is recovering from the accident.

Participles can also have indirect objects as well as direct objects:

Reading **my daughter** a book, I grew sleepy.
Giving **my friend** the news, I chose my words carefully.

Participles can also have direct objects and object complements:

The committee, electing Mrs. Klomstok **chairwoman**, enraged Mr. Lochenhocher.

Participles created from linking verbs can have predicate nominatives or predicate adjectives:

Mr. Dusenberg, being **a wise man**, refused to argue.

Becoming **angry**, Mr. Lochenhocher yelled across the street at Ruthie.

Remaining **calm**, Ruthie continued practicing the bagpipes.

(Notice that *practicing the bagpipes* is a gerund phrase.)

POINTS FOR WRITERS

1. Dangling Participles

As you've just seen, we usually put participles close to the nouns they modify, either before or after. Avoid the infamous **dangling participle**, a carelessly used participial phrase that doesn't apply logically to a nearby noun. The result is often nonsense:

Rowing across the river, the boat struck the ice.
Dancing to the jazz, the orchestra played its closing number.
Falling softly, we watched the snow.
Drinking noisily, Grandmother watched the thirsty dog.

Please don't do this. Please?

EXERCISES

Because students often find verbals difficult, we've provided many different kinds of exercises in this chapter and the next to help you learn these concepts. (Don't thank us; just send money.)

17a. Identify the functions (subjects, direct objects, and others) of the underlined gerunds in these sentences:

1. Farming is his business.

2. His business is farming.

3. He likes farming.

4. He likes raising corn and soy beans.

5. He will stay with farming.

6. His profession, raising corn and soy beans, is a difficult one.

17b. Now locate the gerunds in the following sentences and identify their functions:

1. His hobby is biking.

2. Biking is his hobby.

3. He is interested in biking.

4. His hobby, biking, is a popular one.

5. Biking ten miles a day is a challenge.

6. His goal is biking ten miles a day.

7. He makes time for biking ten miles a day.

8. She likes being a police woman.

9. Being a patrol officer is her ideal job.

Review

Before we go to the next exercises, let's have a quick review.
Gerunds, as we've seen, are present participles used as nouns for many nominal functions:

<u>Running</u> is his hobby.
(A gerund functioning as a subject)

He likes <u>running laps</u>.
(A gerund phrase as a direct object)

Her hobby is <u>playing the tuba</u>.
(A gerund phrase as a predicate nominative)

We also use present participles to create progressive tense verbs, using the verb *to be* as auxiliaries:

He <u>is playing</u> the tuba.

She <u>was</u> always <u>playing</u> the tuba.
I <u>have been playing</u> the tuba.

So gerunds can be distinguished from progressive tense verbs in at least two ways:

1. Gerunds always function as nouns, in a nominal position in the sentence.
2. Progressive tense verbs always have an auxiliary, which is some form of the verb *to be*.

Back to the exercises:

17c. Using the guidelines above, classify the gerunds and progressive verbs in the underlined portions of these sentences:

1. <u>Breathing very cold air</u> can be painful.

2. I love <u>baking cookies</u>.

3. He found much joy in <u>singing</u>.

4. He <u>was singing</u> all the time.

5. You learn a lot from <u>reading books</u>.

6. When you <u>are driving</u>, time passes quickly.

17d. Do the same thing in the following sentences, in which the gerunds and progressive tense verbs are not marked for you:

1. He made a career of programming computers.

2. I was programming computers.

3. Programming is my job.

4. I love juggling.

5. I am juggling all the time.

6. Juggling is what I love to do.

7. Once my hobby was juggling.

Review

Here's another short review concerning verbs and participles:

You will recall that the progressive tense verbs, which use present participles to build verb phrases, use the verb *to be* as auxiliaries:

He <u>is driving</u>.
She <u>was</u> always <u>playing</u> golf.
I <u>will be knitting</u> a sweater.

We also use past participles or present participles to create adjectival phrases that usually appear just before or after the nouns they modify:

<u>Sleeping for hours</u>, John recovered from his cold.
The dog, <u>barking madly</u>, wouldn't be quiet.
<u>Driven to exhaustion</u>, Bob had to rest.

They can also appear after linking verbs:

He seemed <u>disappointed by the news</u>.
He became <u>interested in the new book</u>.

So we can distinguish participles from progressive tense verbs or perfect tense verbs in at least two ways:

1. Participles always function as adjectives and usually appear before or after a noun phrase, or after a linking verb.
2. Progressive tense verbs always have some form of *be* as an auxiliary; perfect tense verbs always have some form of *have* as an auxiliary.

Back to the exercises:

17e. Using the guidelines above, classify the underlined portions of these sentences as participles, as perfect tense verbs, or as progressive tense verbs.

1. Bob <u>was sleeping</u> for hours.

2. Bob, <u>driven to exhaustion</u>, had to rest.

3. Martha <u>has driven</u> Bob to work all week.

4. <u>Swimming laps</u>, Bob begins his day briskly.

5. Bob, <u>biking for miles</u>, was exhausted.

6. <u>Exhausted</u>, Bob nevertheless became <u>intrigued</u>.

7. <u>Driving to work</u>, Martha saw a red fox.

17f. Do the same thing in the following sentences, in which the participles and verbs are not marked for you:

1. Snoring loudly, Susan slept through her history class.

2. Susan was snoring loudly in Calculus.

3. Driven mad by the noise, Claude threw everything in sight.

4. Claude had not slept for two days.

5. Claude appeared worn and worried.

6. Playing the sax, Al woke up the neighbors.

7. Written for Susan, the instructions ordered her to drop her history class.

17g. Using the guidelines discussed in this chapter, classify the underlined portions of the following sentences as gerunds, as participles, as perfect tense verbs, or as progressive tense verbs.

1. His hobby is <u>reading Shakespeare</u>.

2. He <u>is</u> always <u>reading</u> Shakespeare.

3. <u>Reading Shakespeare aloud</u>, he entranced the audience.

4. Alicia, <u>reading Shakespeare</u>, ignored the speaker.

5. <u>Driving at night</u> can be dangerous.

6. I don't like <u>driving at night</u>.

7. <u>Driving late at night</u>, Ed was exhausted.

8. <u>Exhausted</u>, Ed drove on.

9. Ed <u>was driving</u> three nights a week.

10. He <u>has exhausted</u> himself with the <u>driving</u>.

17h. In these sentences, the gerunds, participles, and verbs are not marked for you. Locate and classify the gerunds, participles, perfect tense verbs, and progressive tense verbs:

1. Seen through the window, the room was a mess.

2. We have seen the traffic through the window.

3. My hobby is playing the tuba.

4. Bob is playing the tuba.

5. Playing the tuba, Bob disturbed the library patrons.

6. Feeling sick, Gloria went home.

7. Gloria was feeling sick.

8. Her remarks were about reading Poe.

9. Sailing on the lake is Cal's hobby.

10. I like sailing on the lake.

11. I am sailing again this summer.

18 To Boldly Verb
Infinitives

The third kind of verbal is easy to recognize, but a bit tricky when you analyze its function in a sentence.

INFINITIVES

As we said in Chapter 14, an **infinitive verb** is usually the present form of the verb preceded by the particle *to*: *to laugh, to be, to seem, to break, to pontificate, to discombobulate.* There's an infinitive for every verb in English, except the modal auxiliaries.

But infinitive verbs are never used as a main verb or as an auxiliary verb. Like the other verbals, infinitives perform the functions of other parts of speech, and infinitives are particularly versatile. Infinitives can be used nominally, adjectivally, and adverbially; but, like ordinary verbs, they can still take complements and be modified by adverbs.

First, infinitives can be used nominally, in any way that you'd use a noun:

To quit now would be a mistake.
[a subject]

He likes to run.
[a direct object]

His intention, <u>to explain the law,</u> is reasonable.
[an appositive]

Our goal is <u>to win</u>.
[a predicate nominative]

His intention was <u>to make friends</u>.
[another predicate nominative]

<u>To know her</u> is <u>to trust her</u>.
[a subject *and* a predicate nominative]

Notice that sometimes you can recognize nominal infinitives with this simple test: You can often replace them with gerunds without changing the meaning of the sentence:

<u>To quit now</u> would be a mistake.
<u>Quitting now</u> would be a mistake.

He likes <u>to run</u>.
He likes <u>running</u>.

This test won't work in every instance. It won't work, for example, in *To know her is to trust her.* (We can't say *Knowing her is trusting her.*)

Second, infinitives can be used as adjectives, following a noun or certain linking verbs:

I need a book <u>to read.</u>
[a modifier of *book*]

An opportunity <u>to succeed</u> is a wonderful thing.
[a modifier of *opportunity*]

I'd like a chance <u>to explain</u>.
[a modifier of *chance*]

Notice that in these examples, the infinitives specify the purpose of the nouns they modify: *I need a book.* Why? *I need a book <u>to read</u>.*

The following adjectival infinitives follow linking verbs, and they're both predicate adjectives, describing the subject of the sentence.

He appears <u>to have some money</u>.
They seem <u>to be jerks</u>.

Notice that, in sentences like these, you can often replace the entire infinitive phrase with a roughly synonymous adjective:

He appears <u>wealthy</u>.
They seem <u>arrogant</u>.

Third, infinitives can be used as adverbs, modifying verbs or adjectives. Modifying verbs, the infinitive is often moveable and indicates *how* or *why* the action is performed:

She plays hard <u>to win</u>.
[Why does she play hard?]

<u>To succeed</u>, he studies every day.
[Why does he study?]

<u>To listen well</u>, you need a quiet place.
[Why do you need that quiet place?]

The adverbial infinitives above, like many adverbs and adverbials, are moveable:

<u>To win,</u> she plays hard.
He studies every day <u>to succeed</u>.

Modifying adjectives, the adverbial infinitive appears after the adjective and gives you information about the intent or purpose associated with the modified adjective:

He was ready <u>to study</u>.
[For what was he *ready*?]

I'm happy <u>to help</u>.
[What are you *happy* to do?]

Eager <u>to please</u>, the new employees arrived early.
[What are they *eager* to do?]

Notice that the adverbial infinitives in these last three examples are *not* movable.

In a few cases, infinitives are used without the *to* particle. All of the underlined phrases below are infinitive phrases, but some don't contain the particle:

I want <u>him **to win** the race</u>.
I saw <u>him **win** the race</u>.
I allowed <u>him **to win** the race</u>.
I let <u>him **win** the race</u>.
I'll ask <u>him **to go**</u>.
I'll have <u>him **go**</u>.
I'll force <u>him **to leave**</u>.
I'll make <u>him **leave**</u>.

The absence of the *to* particle is determined by the verb that precedes the infinitive phrase: A small number of transitive verbs (such as *saw, let, make,* and *have*) make the *to* unnecessary—you simply cannot insert *to* into those sentences.

Following most verbs, however, the infinitive must have *to*. (In the exercises in these chapters, we will always use infinitives with the *to* particle.)

By the way, some grammarians call an infinitive that is missing *to* a *bare infinitive* (which is about as risqué as grammarians ever get).

Like gerunds and participles, infinitives can be used with direct objects, with adverbs, and with other grammatical entities associated with the verb. (See the examples above wherein *the race* is a direct object.)

Infinitives can even have subjects, which perform the action of the infinitive:

I like **my children** to read every day.
[*My children* is the subject of the infinitive; they do the reading. *Every day* is an adverbial phrase.]

I like **Kelly** to enjoy these nightly readings.
[*Kelly* is the subject of the infinitive verb; she does the enjoying. *These nightly readings* is the direct object of *to enjoy*.]

I need **you** to go to the store today.
[*You* is the subject; *to the store* and *today* are adverbial, modifying the infinitive.]

I want **her** to enjoy reading.
[*Her* is the subject of the infinitive; *reading*, a gerund, is the direct object of the infinitive.]

Notice the last example above: When a pronoun precedes the infinitive as the subject of that infinitive, it will (strangely) be in the objective case:

I like **them** to read every day.
I need **him** to go to the store today.
I want **us** to enjoy reading.

PASSIVE INFINITIVES

All the infinitives we've seen so far are linking or intransitive, or they are transitive and active. But there are other forms.

A less often used but important variant is the *passive infinitive*, constructed with the infinitive of *be* (i.e., *to be*) followed by the past participle of a main verb (*to be recognized, to be known, to be continued*).

In these examples, nominal passive infinitives follow transitive verbs and function as direct objects:

I'm nervous about my surgery, so I prefer to be driven to the hospital.

I needed to be helped, but no one was nearby.

He has longed to be recognized by his colleagues for his contributions.

He did not expect to be apprehended by the authorities for his misdeeds.

These passive infinitives are subjects:

To be recognized for his contributions was his goal.
To be apprehended was his fear.

Passive infinitives can also be predicate nominatives and appositives:

His goal was <u>to be recognized for his efforts</u>.
He never achieved his goal, <u>to be recognized for his work</u>.

And there are also adverbial passive infinitives. In the following examples, the adverbial passives are moveable:

<u>To be prepared for your finals</u>, study throughout the semester.
<u>To be found</u>, the lost hiker built a fire on the hill.

And in the next examples, the adverbial passive infinitives modify the adjectives preceding them:

She was ready <u>to be tested</u>.
They were eager <u>to be heard</u>.

PERFECT INFINITIVES

The infrequently used *perfect infinitive* is constructed with the auxiliary *have* (never *has* or *had*) followed by the past participle of a main verb (*to have known, to have seen, to have continued*), as in these examples of nominal perfect infinitives used as subjects:

<u>To have known Lincoln</u> would be remarkable.

<u>To have heard him deliver the Gettysburg Address</u> would be thrilling.

<u>To have continued performing the play after the announcement</u> was impossible.

These perfect infinitive phrases are direct objects:

The police did not expect <u>to have apprehended the criminal by this time</u>.

We had hoped <u>to have seen our new nephew</u> by this time.

Perfect infinitives can be adverbial, too:

They are known <u>to have lived here for many years</u>.

We seldom encounter the passive and perfect infinitives because we usually express the idea in some simpler way: *People know that they lived here for many years.*

There are still other, even rarer, forms of the infinitive: They can be perfect progressive (*to have been speaking*) and passive perfect (*to have been shown*), but we had hoped *to have been finished* with this topic by now.

POINTS FOR WRITERS

1. The split infinitive.

One of the best-known rules of prescriptive grammar says that we must not split infinitives. That is, we must not put an adverb between *to* and the verb:

He wants <u>to quickly finish</u> college.
He wants <u>to finish</u> college <u>quickly</u>.

Work hard <u>to gradually improve</u> your writing.
Work hard <u>to improve</u> your writing <u>gradually</u>.

As the second example in each pair demonstrates, it's usually easy to fix a split infinitive. In some contexts, however, many writers occasionally and judiciously do the splits. As in all good writing, tread carefully.

2. Go dangle your infinitives elsewhere, bub.

There can be dangling infinitives, which, like dangling participles, do not clearly or logically work with the rest of the sentence. A passive verb elsewhere in the clause often creates this problem:

<u>To get to the market today</u>, your chores **should be done** early.

<u>To be heard in this large room</u>, the microphone **must be adjusted**.

Make the independent clause active, and the infinitive phrase usually makes better sense:

<u>To get to the market today</u>, you **should do** your chores early.
<u>To be heard in this large room</u>, we **must adjust** the microphone.

Respectable people never dangle their infinitives (at least, not in public).

EXERCISES

18a. Identify the function of the nominal infinitives in these sentences:

1. <u>To become a star</u> was her adolescent dream.

2. She wants <u>to become a star</u>.

3. Her dream, <u>to become a star</u>, may never come true.

4. <u>To live</u> is <u>to dream</u>.

5. <u>To know him</u> is <u>to love him</u>.

6. I'd like him to do the project.

7. He'll ask her to help.

8. I'm hoping for them to succeed.

18b. Locate the nominal infinitive phrases in these sentences and identify their functions:

1. I need to get some water.

2. To succeed requires hard work.

3. To discipline yourself means to make sacrifices. [Hint: *means* is a linking verb here.]

4. He explained his goal, to become fluent in German.

5. He wants to see me in the morning.

6. It won't be hard for him to see me then.

7. Would you like to see me, too?

8. There's time for me to see you.

18c. Identify the functions of the adjectival infinitives in these sentences: What words do they modify?

1. I have the tools to get the job done.

2. Time to use the tools is what I need now.

3. Something to open the tool packages would be handy now.

4. A scissors <u>to open this</u> would be helpful.

5. I could help if I had some dynamite <u>to open this</u>.

6. I need a screwdriver <u>to loosen this</u>.

7. A screwdriver <u>to loosen this</u> would help.

8. The tool I need, a screwdriver <u>to loosen this</u>, is not here.

18d. Locate the adjectival infinitives in these sentences and identify the words they modify:

1. Every day we send urgent messages to complain about the service.

2. She bought me a carry-on bag to take on my trip.

3. Someone to guide me on the way would be helpful.

4. I found someone to guide you.

5. To relax, he needed a book to interest him.

6. All she asked for was a book to read, a place in which to stay warm, and something to eat.

18e. Identify the functions of the adverbial infinitives in these sentences: What words do they modify?

1. <u>To relax</u>, he sang.

2. He read the book <u>to please his daughter.</u>

3. <u>To please his daughter</u>, he read the book.

4. <u>To become a fireman</u>, the young man studied and trained.

5. The young man studied and trained <u>to become a fireman</u>.

6. He was eager <u>to become a fireman</u>.

7. We were happy <u>to help him</u>.

8. He was careful <u>to speak with me beforehand</u>.

18f. Yet again, locate the adverbial infinitives here and identify the words they modify:

1. You need a telescope to be an astronomer.

2. He was ready to be an astronomer.

3. She was determined to be an astronomer.

4. Eager to play ball, the team waited.

5. Happy to see her friend, Julie cried.

6. Reluctant to go, the children fidgeted.

7. We were sorry to leave.

8. She rose to leave.

18g. Identify all the infinitive phrases, with complements and modifiers, in these sentences and classify them as nominal, adjectival, or adverbial:

1. That child needs me to look after her.

2. To succeed, you have to work hard.

3. I'm looking for a place to sit down.

4. To be blunt, I will say that I'm angry at you.

5. He is trying to impress his boss.

6. I am not here to impress anyone.

7. His reason, to impress his boss, is sufficient.

8. His goal is to impress his boss.

9. We want her to come to the party.

10. We hope she'd like to come to the party.

18h. In the following pairs of sentences, read the first sentence and then, using the first sentence as a clue, analyze the grammar in the underlined verbal phrase in the second sentence.
An example:

Randolph likes Italian food.
Randolph likes <u>to eat Italian food</u>.

Because *likes* is a transitive verb, we can reason that, in the first sentence, *Italian food* is a direct object. So the infinitive phrase in the second sentence must also be a direct object.

1. He likes mystery novels.
   He likes <u>to read mystery novels</u>.

2. He reads them before school.
   He likes <u>reading them before school</u>.

3. She is quite ready.
   She is ready <u>to sing</u>.

4. She is very happy.
   She is happy <u>to sing</u>.

5. The smiling opera star took center stage.
   <u>Singing the aria loudly</u>, the opera star took center stage.

6. He annoys us.
   <u>His singing arias at 6 a.m.</u> annoys us.

7. I don't enjoy opera at 6 a.m.
   I don't enjoy <u>listening to opera</u> at 6 a.m.

8. I want music at any time.
   I want <u>to listen to opera</u> at any time.

18i. Identify the underlined verbals as gerunds, participles, or infinitives. Then identify the function that the verbal performs in each sentence.

1. He likes <u>to read</u>.

2. He likes <u>reading novels</u>.

3. <u>Running quickly</u>, he soon arrived at home.

4. His <u>singing</u> annoyed us.

5. <u>Known to the entire community</u>, the mayor is respected.

6. The silent film star, <u>seen but never recognized</u>, lived in our neighborhood.

7. He wants <u>to earn money</u>.

8. He writes <u>to learn</u>.

9. They were prepared <u>to fight</u>.

10. <u>To succeed</u>, you must be prepared <u>to work hard</u>.

19 What's *That?*
More Pronouns

We have already learned about two important groups of pronouns: the **personal pronouns** and the **relative pronouns**. In this chapter, we'll examine the four other groups, which, though perhaps not as prominent in some grammars, are words that we need every day.

These pronouns are tricky to discuss in an orderly way because grammarians have different ways of sorting them out, and some pronouns fit into two or more categories, depending on the way we use them. (There's that *form* and *function* idea again.) The relative pronoun *who* can also be an interrogative pronoun. The relative pronoun *that* can also be a demonstrative pronoun. So it goes.

THE REFLEXIVE PRONOUNS

The **reflexive pronouns** are compound words. In each one, the first part is a personal pronoun and the second part is always *–self*. They are often used for emphasis:

I'll do the job myself!
All right, do it yourself.
He really should do it himself.
We should all do it ourselves.
She herself told them to do it themselves!

Notice that in all the examples above, the reflexive pronouns are redundant—without them, the sentences would communicate the same meanings, but less emphatically. When used this way, the *–self* pronouns are often called *intensifying pronouns*. (In the last example above, by the way, *herself* is an appositive for *she*.)

Just as often, reflexive pronouns communicate something about the subjects of the sentence performing actions upon themselves—making the action reflexive:

Jim hurt <u>himself</u>.
June found <u>herself</u> in an enviable situation.
Emily and Roy removed <u>themselves</u> from the competition.
Well, this vase didn't break <u>itself</u>.

A bit later we will examine the indefinite pronouns, including *one*. We mention it here because *one* has the reflexive *oneself* (which is sometimes written *one's self*):

One should take care of <u>oneself</u>.

As you see, the reflexive pronouns can be in the first, second, or third person. When the first part is plural, the second part is, too. That is, there is no *ourself* or *themself,* although you may sometimes hear people say those words. (There is also no *hisself*, but you'll hear that, too.)

Use *yourself* or *yourselves* as the context requires.

THE DEMONSTRATIVE PRONOUNS

Demonstrative pronouns are four common and easy pronouns (usually used nominally, but sometimes adjectivally) that call attention to the antecedents. They are typically present in the immediate verbal or physical context:

<u>This</u> is the guilty person!
<u>That</u> is the murderer!
<u>These</u> are his victims!
<u>Those</u> were his motives!
He used <u>these</u> weapons on <u>those</u> victims for <u>that</u> reason!
Officer, arrest <u>this</u> man!

These pronouns (*that's* another one!) direct the audience's attention to a particular word in the verbal context, or to a person or thing in the physical context.

THE INTERROGATIVE PRONOUNS

There are also the five familiar **interrogative pronouns**, which we use in questions every day:

<u>Who</u> threw that pie?
<u>Which</u> of you bozos threw that?
At <u>whom</u> did he throw that?
<u>Whose</u> meringue pie was thrown?
Hey, <u>what</u> happened to my pie?

Notice that these five are identical to the five relative pronouns—except for the relative *that*, which has been replaced by *what*.

As the examples show, these words (except the possessive *whose*) usually fill a nominal function in questions. In that way, they enable us to ask questions that can be answered with a noun.

Several *–ever* pronouns (*whoever, whichever,* and *whatever*) can also be used as interrogative pronouns:

<u>Whoever</u> would throw my pie?
<u>Whatever</u> caused him to do it?

THE INDEFINITE PRONOUNS

The last and largest of the pronoun classes are the **indefinite pronouns**, which are indefinite because they are typically used without any clear, specific antecedents. They are sometimes organized into several overlapping groups.

There is usually little point in learning these subclasses of indefinite pronouns, but the subclasses give us a way to discuss these pronouns in an organized fashion.

The Indefinite Singulars:

These include the *-body*, *-one*, and *-thing* pronouns, and several negative pronouns:

Anybody, everybody, somebody, nobody
Anyone, everyone, someone, no one
Anything, everything, something, nothing

Among the indefinite singulars are also *each*, *one*, *another*, and *none*, and *either* and *neither*:

<u>Everyone</u> can have some dinner.
<u>Each</u> of us should have some.
<u>No one</u> will be left out.
<u>Everybody</u> will get plenty.
Hey, I've got plenty of <u>nothing</u>.

The Indefinite Plurals:

These are *any*, *some*, and *all; both*, *few*, and *several;* and *enough, plenty,* and *more*.

<u>All</u> of us are responsible.
<u>Some</u> of us should accept responsibility.
At least a <u>few</u> accepted it.
Well, <u>more</u> should accept it.

Many are called, but few are chosen.

The Indefinite Portions:

These are all singular, and they all refer to a portion of something that cannot be counted out, but only measured in quantities, like Jell-O or mashed potatoes: *all* and *none; little* and *less; much* and *more;* and *some, enough,* and *plenty.*

Have you had some?
Yes, but I'll take more.
You should take less.
Hey, I've *still* got plenty of nothing.
Well, nothing is plenty for you (said Porgy).

While the personal pronouns have a special possessive form, the possessives of some indefinite pronouns are formed by adding –'s: *one's, everyone's, nobody's.*

When *else* follows a pronoun (as in *anybody else, everyone else,* or *no one else*), it is considered part of the pronoun. In those cases, the possessive is formed by adding –'s to *else: anybody else's, everyone else's,* and *no one else's*:

Do all these pronouns make anybody else's head hurt?

Still Others:

Some authorities include among these indefinite pronouns a few words that we've seen before, the **compound pronouns** based on *-ever: whoever, whomever, whichever,* and *whatever.*

Like the preceding indefinite pronouns, the *-ever* pronouns can be used in statements containing no explicit antecedent—and are often used when the writer or speaker does not know the antecedent:

<u>Whoever</u> made this mess must clean it up!
You can choose <u>whichever</u> you like.
<u>Whatever</u> it is (Groucho once said), I'm against it.

Similarly, the **reciprocal pronouns** may be indefinite or may refer to specific people, depending on the context.

There are only two reciprocals: *each other* and *one another*. By the strictest rules of usage, *each other* is used to refer to two people; *one another* should be used for three or more:

The Diefenbacher twins are always arguing with <u>each other</u>.

"If God loved us, my dear friends, we also must love <u>one another</u>." (1 John 4: 11)

Finally, *it* (also a personal pronoun) is sometimes an indefinite pronoun, used idiomatically to refer vaguely to weather, general circumstances, or some unspecified subject in the context:

<u>It</u> may rain.
You could master any foreign language if you kept at <u>it</u>.
Whatever <u>it</u> is (Groucho said again), I'm against <u>it</u>.
"So <u>it</u> goes," said Mr. Vonnegut.

And, even more finally, many of the words in this chapter are also used adjectivally as well as nominally:

<u>This</u> door; <u>that</u> door.
<u>Some</u> doors; <u>all</u> doors.
<u>Few</u> doors; <u>one</u> door.

POINTS FOR WRITERS

1. They are everywhere.

Sometimes, especially in casual conversation and careless writing, we use *they* as an indefinite pronoun, referring (often negatively) to unspecified groups of people:

<u>They</u> are all against me!
<u>They</u> are all part of a plot!
And, furthermore, <u>they</u> think I'm paranoid!

Avoid this vague, careless, and indefinite use of *they* (or they will get you).

2. Redundant reflexives.

Sometimes reflexive pronouns are absolutely necessary, as with certain verbs:

I pride <u>myself</u> on my knowledge of geography.

But we often use reflexives unnecessarily:

I <u>myself</u> prefer my coffee black.

Using unnecessary reflexives is not a terrible error, but it doesn't contribute anything to a sentence, either.

3. The number of none.

Traditionally *none* has been declared a singular pronoun. Today *none* is often accepted as singular or plural, as the context and the writer's intention require:

<u>None</u> of the players is [*or* are] here.

EXERCISES

19a. We've examined four classes of pronouns in this chapter. Write the names of the four classes and check your list by looking back through the chapter.

19b. Now, for each of the four classes, write as many pronouns as you can remember. Check your lists by looking back and write down those you forgot.

19c. Write one sentence that contains an example of each of the four classes you listed above. Compare your sentences with the examples in this chapter.

19d. Each of the following sentences contains at least one example of the pronouns described in this chapter. Classify each underlined example.

1. <u>What</u> are you doing?

2. <u>Who</u> wants to know?

3. <u>That</u> is the dumbest question <u>anyone</u> ever asked.

4. I <u>myself</u> am going to teach you some manners because you obviously have <u>none</u>.

5. <u>Both</u> of you need to stop <u>this</u> immediately.

6. I doubt that you can do <u>anything</u> to stop us.

7. <u>Whatever</u> could you do?

8. <u>Anybody</u> who tries to stop me is going to get <u>it</u>.

9. Can't <u>someone</u> do <u>something</u> to help me?

10. I've had <u>enough</u> of <u>all</u> of you.

(Pronouns bring out the worst in some people.)

20 Many Things
(But no Cabbages or Kings)

In this book, we don't try to cover every possible topic in English grammar, but here are a few that we still need to discuss briefly.

THE EXPLETIVE *IT*

The personal pronoun *it* can be used as an expletive (as *there* is used), to postpone the subject until later in the sentence. The subject will then appear later in the sentence, usually to the right of the verb.

The expletive *it* can only work with a subject that is a nominal infinitive phrase or a nominal clause.

The expletive *it* is used less frequently than *there*, appearing in sentences similar to the following pairs, where the first sentence in each pair contains no expletive. All the subjects are underlined.

<u>To admit my mistakes</u> is difficult.
It is difficult <u>to admit my mistakes</u>.

<u>That I made mistakes</u> is true.
It is true <u>that I made mistakes</u>.

As we've seen, the phrase *to admit my mistakes* is called a verbal (more specifically, a nominal infinitive phrase). And *that I made mistakes* is a nominal clause.

Like the expletive *there*, expletive *it* has no grammatical function in these sentences, only a stylistic function: to postpone the appearance of the subject. In the following pairs of sentences, the grammatical structure is exactly the same in both sentences, and the underlined portions are the subjects.

<u>To trust him</u> is difficult.
It is difficult <u>to trust him</u>.

<u>To understand the theory</u> requires patience.
It requires patience <u>to understand the theory</u>.

<u>That the universe is expanding</u> is a fact.
It is a fact <u>that the universe is expanding</u>.

<u>That you have worked hard</u> became apparent.
It became apparent <u>that you have worked hard</u>.

When we write sentences like these, we typically write the versions with the expletive *it*; the versions without *it* sometimes seem awkward.

In English, we also use the pronoun *it* as a subject in conventional expressions regarding weather or time. In these sentences, *it* is an indefinite pronoun, not an expletive:

<u>It</u> may rain today.
<u>It</u> is about four pm.

Don't confuse the pronoun *it* with the expletive *it* that postpones the subject. If there is no nominal clause or infinitive phrase later in the sentence, *it* is a pronoun, not an expletive.

SENTENCE MODIFIERS

Sentence modifiers are words, phrases, or clauses that don't modify any particular word in the sentence. Instead they modify the entire sentence in an unusual way, by indicating the writer's attitude or intention about the sentence. The following sentences begin with sentence modifiers:

<u>Clearly</u>, he's a fool.
<u>Frankly</u>, he's a fool.
<u>Sadly</u>, he's a fool.
<u>To tell the truth</u>, so are you.

Sentence modifiers are concise ways of saying things that would otherwise require more words, even an entire additional clause.

If we rewrote the sentences above without sentence modifiers, we would produce the following sentences (or something like them):

<u>It is clear to me that</u> he's a fool.
<u>I speak frankly when I say that</u> he's a fool.
<u>I am sad to observe that</u> he's a fool.
<u>I tell the truth when I say that</u> you are, too.

Sentence modifiers often appear at the beginning of sentences, but, like adverbs, they can be placed elsewhere. Notice, in all the examples in this section, the placement of commas:

So, <u>to tell the truth</u>, are you.
So are you, <u>to tell the truth</u>.

It's easy to mistake sentence modifiers for adverbs. Keep in mind that true adverbs will modify some specific word or phrase in the sentence: a verb, adjective, or another adverb. This sentence contains an adverb, modifying the phrasal verb *laid out*:

Mark <u>honestly</u> laid out his plans.

But this sentence contains a sentence modifier that reveals the attitude of the writer:

<u>Honestly</u>, Mark laid out his plans quite well.

Similarly, don't mistake dangling participles (or any participles) for sentence modifiers:

<u>Speaking frankly</u>, Michael criticized the plan.
[A participle, modifying *Michael*]

<u>Frankly</u>, this plan looks impractical.
[A sentence modifier]

This next example is ambiguous when out of context: It could contain a dangling participle or a sentence modifier that looks like a dangling participle. In either case, it probably needs rewriting: delete *speaking*.

<u>Speaking frankly</u>, Michael's criticisms seemed reasonable.

ABSOLUTE PHRASES

An **absolute phrase**, sometimes called a *nominative absolute*, is a noun phrase often followed by a modifier (a participial phrase, a prepositional phrase, or other adjectivals):

<u>The sun having set</u>, Dracula considered where he might have breakfast.

Some grammarians call these phrases *absolute*, meaning that the phrases are independent from the rest of the sentence; they are said to play no grammatical role in the sentence.

But in these chapters, we consider absolutes as noun phrases used adverbially, telling us *when, where, why,* or *how* the action of the verb is performed:

> <u>Dr. Seward being out of town</u>, I will sign the forms for him.
> <u>The classrooms infested with spiders</u>, we called Renfield.
> Harker, <u>his hands trembling</u>, stepped into his English classroom.

This simple test for absolutes may be helpful: If the sentence still means the same thing after you've added the preposition *with* to the beginning of the noun phrase, the noun phrase is very probably an absolute:

> [With] <u>the classrooms infested with spiders</u>, we called Renfield.
> [With] <u>Renfield taking care of the spiders</u>, we left for lunch.

VERBS HAVE MOODS

Earlier we discussed the four-way classification of sentences according to their purposes: the declarative, interrogative, imperative, and exclamatory sentences.

Verbs are an important part of that classification, and a related quality of verbs in those kinds of sentences is called modality, expressed by the **mood** of a verb in certain sentences. Grammarians have discussed and classified verb moods in several ways, but, generally, English verbs are said to have four moods, three of them corresponding with the classifications of sentence purpose:

- Verbs in the **indicative mood** are those that appear in declarative sentences (*Joshua went away*).
- Verbs in the **interrogative mood** appear in interrogative sentences (*Did Joshua go?*). The use of the *do* auxiliary in questions is often a mark of the interrogative mood.
- Verbs in the **imperative mood** appear in imperative sentences (*Go away!*). The disappearance of the subject and some auxiliaries is often a mark of the imperative.

Exclamatory sentences, as we saw, have no special form or structure.

There's a fourth mood, and it's the important one at the moment because it's useful in creating sentences that don't correspond neatly to the four-way classification:

- Verbs in the **conditional mood** express necessity and possibility.

We create verbs in the conditional mood using a subset of the auxiliary verbs that are called the **modal auxiliaries**:

can and *could*
shall and *should*
will and *would*
may, must, and *might*

(By the way, these modal auxiliaries are the verbs that *don't* have principal parts or infinitives.)

These modal auxiliary verbs are always the first auxiliary in the complete verb, and they help us discuss various kinds of necessary, possible, or permitted actions. Notice the differences (some subtle) among these sentences:

I <u>can</u> go to the store.
I <u>shall</u> go to the store.
I <u>will</u> go to the store.
I <u>may</u> go to the store.
I <u>might</u> go to the store.

I <u>could</u> go to the store.
I <u>should</u> go to the store.
I <u>would</u> go to the store.
I <u>must</u> go to the store.

Often we clarify and reinforce the conditional nature of these sentences with some modifier or additional clause, as in *I <u>could</u> go to the store if I <u>may</u> borrow your car.*

Notice that all of the sentences above are in some way about *future* possible events. So it's not surprising that one of the modal auxiliaries that we use often is *will*, because (as we've seen) we use it for future-tense verbs: *will drive, will have driven, will be driving.*

This has had interesting consequences for another modal, *shall*, which we don't use much any more.

According to prescriptive grammars, *shall* should be used for future tenses only when the subject is in the first person; *will* should be reserved for future tenses when the subject is second- or third-person:

Today <u>I shall read</u> that article.
Today <u>they will read</u> that article.

This conservative use of *will* and *shall* also prescribes that *will* should be used for the first person and *shall* for the second and third persons when we express an emphatic *determination* to perform a future action:

You may try to stop me, but <u>I *will* read</u> that article.
You may try to stop them, but <u>they *shall* read</u> that article.

Because many U. S. readers and writers are unaware of these distinctions, writers commonly use *will* in many cases where we once used *shall*. But *shall* is still preserved in some contexts, as in certain questions: *Shall we move on now? Let's continue, shall we?*

Another careful distinction is sometimes made between the auxiliaries *may* and *might*, recognizing *might* as the past tense of *may*. This distinction is today seldom recognized, but is still used as in these sentences:

> I <u>may be</u> able to help if I have the time.
> Last week I <u>might have been</u> able to help.

YA REALLY OUGHTA READ THIS

Ought to (as in *You ought to pipe down*) is considered an unusual modal auxiliary—by some people. That requires some explanation.

Ought is an archaic form of our verb *owed* (past tense of *owe*), so it was once used as a transitive main verb.

Today *ought to* is used—some believe—as an unusual two-word modal auxiliary, roughly synonymous with *should*, as in *You should* [or *ought to*] *pipe down*, or *That statement should* [or *ought to*] *be enough*. (Some dictionaries and grammars draw fine distinctions between the meanings of *ought* and *should* that need not concern us here.)

In this analysis, *ought to* is followed by a present, perfect, or progressive tense verb, or a passive verb:

> You <u>ought to</u> see
> You <u>ought to</u> have seen
> You <u>ought to</u> be seeing
> You <u>ought to</u> be seen

Others argue that *ought* is still a transitive main verb, followed by an infinitive verb beginning, as usual, with *to*. In this case, *ought* is similar to other transitive verbs that can be followed by infinitives, like *have* or *need*. We learned about such structures in Chapters 17 and 18:

> You ought <u>to see</u> (compare *have to see* or *need to see*)
> You ought <u>to have seen</u> (*have to have seen* or *need to have seen*)
> You ought <u>to be seeing</u> (*have to be seeing* or *need to be seeing*)
> You ought <u>to be seen</u> (*have to be seen* or *need to be seen*)

If this analysis is correct, we again notice that infinitives can have perfect, progressive, or passive forms.

We form negative uses of this verb by simply inserting *not* immediately after *ought*, as Rubeus Hagrid kindly demonstrates in the first of the *Harry Potter* books:

> Now listen to me, all three of you, you're meddling in things that <u>ought not to</u> be meddled in.

In examples like this, the placement of *not* suggests (but does not *prove*) that *ought to* isn't a grammatical unit (because it's interrupted by *not*), and that the *to* belongs to the following verb. In other words, sentences like Hagrid's use may be evidence that *ought* is a transitive main verb, followed by an infinitive.

A counter-argument might be that *ought*, considered as a main present-tense verb (*Today you ought to clean your room*), is strange indeed, for it has no progressive form (*oughting*?). This suggests that *ought* is an auxiliary, because some other auxiliaries lack progressive forms (i.e., there is no *musting* or *shalling*).

The disagreement among grammarians will surely go on, and we ought not to get involved.

THE SUBJUNCTIVE MOOD

Another mood grammarians sometimes identify (they have more moods than a thirteen-year-old) is the **subjunctive mood**. It appears in statements about hypothetical situations: e.g., suggestions, wishes, speculations, and prayers. The verb is usually the same as in the indicative mood, but in some cases, especially using the verb *to be*, there's a difference. The subjunctive often appears in traditional or conventional sentences:

Blessed <u>be</u> the name of the Lord!
I move that this meeting <u>be</u> adjourned.

Sometimes we combine the subjunctive in one clause with the conditional mood in another clause:

If I <u>were</u> you, I <u>would tell</u> him off.
If he <u>weren't</u> so lazy, he <u>could be</u> a millionaire.

Increasingly in present-day English, we don't use distinctly subjunctive verbs. Instead we rely on other means to express the hypothetical nature of these ideas. Compare these pairs of sentences, in which the first sentence is in the subjunctive mood:

I suggest that Ed <u>drop</u> the matter.
I think that Ed <u>should drop</u> the matter.

If Dad <u>were</u> here, he would know what to do.
If Dad <u>was</u> here, he would know what to do.

The use of *was* in the last example is now regarded by many as acceptable, and the *If* indicates the hypothetical nature of the first clause.

EXERCISES

20a. In the following multiple-choice questions, classify the underlined words. You will use some answers more than once; you may not need some answers at all.

A. Expletive
B. Noun of direct address
C. Appositive
D. Subject of the sentence
E. Sentence modifier

1. <u>It</u> was surprising to hear the news.

2. It was surprising <u>to hear the news</u>.

3. <u>It</u> is time to go.

4. Gosh, <u>John</u>, you forgot your shoes.

5. <u>Frankly</u>, John often forgets his shoes.

6. <u>It</u> is amazing that you forgot your shoes.

7. You can speak with Mr. Smith, <u>the principal</u>.

8. <u>Truly</u>, Mr. Smith is a patient man.

20b. Underline the absolute phrases in the following sentences:

The sun having set, we walked home.

Our faces wet and cold, we arrived at my parents' house.

20c. Now combine the following pairs of sentences into single sentences, rewriting the first sentence as an absolute phrase. <u>Underline</u> the absolute phrase:

Our time was running short. We hurried to the station.

Her suitcase was safely stowed away. June finally relaxed.

Our last obstacle was overcome. We all relaxed.

20d. List the five moods of verbs.

20e. List the nine modal auxiliaries.

21 Keeping Those Little Puncs in Line

A Brief Review of Punctuation

Many of the basic rules of punctuation are probably second nature to you, and so you know the common uses of periods, question marks, and other marks. In this chapter, we'll discuss others, including many we use every day, about which you may not be certain. If you need help with the grammatical terms, see the glossary or the index.

We won't attempt to explain the various and conflicting rules of punctuation in the several different systems for documenting research: MLA, APA, Chicago, and others. For those, consult the relevant guidebooks and websites. In this chapter, when we use quotations in examples, we omit citations.

We'll start with an easy one.

ADDRESSING ENVELOPES

The U. S. Postal Service now requests all capital letters and no punctuation in addresses on envelopes:

MR VERBAL MORTON
2244 PROPERNOUN ST
CONJUNCTION JUNCTION MA 01001

Addresses like this are easier for their mechanized sorters to read (http://pe.usps.com/BusinessMail101?ViewName=DeliveryAddress).

APOSTROPHES

Many people are confused by the uses of apostrophes showing possession. One reason for the confusion is that possessive apostrophes are often omitted in signs: e.g., *McDonalds*.

The rules are, with one exception, easy:

1. Apostrophes show contraction of personal pronouns and verbs; of verbs and *not*; and of nouns and verbs:

    Heather's car—it's gone, isn't it?

    Heather's upset, isn't she?

2. Possessive pronouns (like *his, hers, its, yours,* and *theirs*) never contain apostrophes. We are particularly likely to forget this when we're using *its* (the possessive pronoun) and *it's* (the contraction for *it is*).

3. Plural possessives that end in –*s* take an apostrophe and no additional *s*: *supervisors', librarians', soldiers'*.
    Plurals that don't end in –*s* take both the apostrophe and –*s* to show possession: *media's, criteria's*.

4. There is no consensus on punctuating some possessives. Some authorities (like the Modern Language Association, and Strunk and White) call for –*'s* after all singular nouns to form possessives, including nouns that end in –*s*: *Clemens's, Dickens's, Jesus's*.
    Other authorities (like the *Associated Press Stylebook* and the American Psychological Association) omit the final –*s* in

those possessives: *Clemens', Dickens', Jesus'.* Find out which style you're required to use and learn it.

5. Similarly, some authorities call for apostrophes to make certain unusual plurals:

> He wants to earn all <u>A's and B's</u> this semester.
> He prefers the jazz from the <u>1940's</u>.

More and more, it has become acceptable to omit the apostrophes here: *He earned As and Bs; the 1940s.* But used carelessly, the omission can be momentarily confusing. For example, the plural *As* could be confused with the conjunction *as.* Follow your teachers' (or supervisors') preferences on these.

COMMAS

The Parenthetical Commas

Commas often come in pairs, like parentheses, and these pairs have a good many uses. In general, we can use them where we might use a pair of parentheses (or a pair of dashes).

With parenthetical commas, the most common and serious error is forgetting the second comma. Don't do that.

1. Put a pair of commas where you could put parentheses. For example, put a pair of commas around an appositive:

> Mr. Smith **(**<u>the principal</u>**)** went to talk to the family.
> Mr. Smith**,** <u>the principal</u>**,** has returned.

2. Put a pair of commas around a parenthetical comment (one that interrupts the sentence):

That Bliebermeier boy (whom I've pointed out before) is a curious kid.

That Bliebermeier boy, the one I mentioned previously, has been staring at me.

3. Place commas around states (in city-state phrases) and years (in month-day-year phrases):

Salem, Massachusetts, is my favorite city.
Salem, Massachusetts, USA, is my favorite city.

October 1939 is when my grandfather was born.
[No commas are necessary.]

October 31, 1938, is the day the Martians landed in Grover's Mill, New Jersey, and abducted Orson Welles.

4. A pair of commas typically encloses adjectives that follow a noun:

The audience, skeptical and snide, refused to believe my story about Orson Welles.

Single Commas

For several reasons, it's easy to be confused about single commas. Unlike most punctuation, commas have a variety of uses, and some of those uses are optional. Different professions and disciplines (like journalism) have their own rules about some uses.

We'll explain a set of common uses.

1. Use a comma after a coordinating conjunction that joins two independent clauses:

He got the job at the bookstore**,** <u>and</u> he means to keep it.
He intended to keep the job**,** <u>but</u> then he found a better one.

We're allowed to omit the comma if the clauses are short and easy to understand without it:

He's employed and he means to stay employed.

2. In a sentence that begins with a subordinate clause, add a comma at the end of the subordinate clause:

   <u>Because Mortimer was late</u>**,** the boss docked his pay.
   <u>Before he docked Mortimer's pay</u>**,** the boss spoke with him.

   If the subordinate clause is short (no more than three or four words long), the comma may be omitted. If we write the sentences above with the independent clause first, no comma is necessary.

   The boss docked Mortimer's pay <u>because he was late</u>.
   The boss spoke with Mortimer <u>after he docked his pay</u>.

3. Use a comma whenever you need one for clarity. Consider this sentence:

   WRONG: Some authorities (like the Modern Language Association and Strunk and White) call for –'s after all singular nouns to form possessives.

   The phrase *the Modern Language Association and Strunk and White* is momentarily confusing: *Strunk and White* might be read as one authority or two. The comma prevents confusion:

RIGHT: Some authorities (like the Modern Language Association, and Strunk and White) call for –'s after all singular nouns to form possessives.

4. Here's a general rule for single commas that's helpful: Never place just one comma between the subject and verb of the sentence:

WRONG: <u>Nancy,</u> is the best treasurer we've ever had.
[*Nancy* is the subject, so no comma is needed.]

WRONG: Nancy, <u>the treasurer</u> is not here today.
[Two commas are needed around *the treasurer*, which is an appositive.]

RIGHT: <u>Ed,</u> did you know that Nancy is the treasurer?
[This is correct because *Ed* is a noun of direct address, not the subject.]

5. We use commas to separate items in a series:

His favorite necktie is <u>blue, green, red, and gray</u>.

But there is disagreement about that last comma (the one before *and*), which is known as the *serial comma* (and also as the *Oxford* comma and *that infernal* comma). Some authorities leave it out unless it's necessary for clarity. Others prefer to use it consistently. Learn which style your teacher or editor prefers.

Commas and Non-restrictive Modifiers

Use commas around non-restrictive modifiers, including clauses. This point may call for a bit of review:

Restrictive clauses (you'll recall) are adjectivals that contain necessary information that helps to define the noun; they *restrict* (or narrow down) the meaning of the modified noun to something more specific. They are *never* enclosed in commas.

Non-restrictive clauses don't narrow down, or restrict, the meaning of the noun; they simply provide supplementary information. They are always enclosed by commas.

Restrictive: All politicians who are crooks should be jailed.

Non-restrictive: All politicians, who are crooks, should be jailed.

The first example above says something about *only* those specific politicians who are crooks. The second says that *all* politicans should be jailed because they are *all* crooks.

The commas mark the difference in meaning. (Notice that you could also use a pair of parentheses in the second sentence, instead of commas.)

SEMI-COLONS

These are generally easier than commas: We use them in only a few cases.

1. Use a semi-colon—and no coordinating conjunction—to join two independent clauses into one sentence:

    Jill likes the human anatomy class**;** she doesn't need it for her major, however.

    If both clauses are simple and brief, and neither contains commas, you are allowed to join them with a comma:

It's not the heat, it's the humidity.

2. Use semi-colons to join two or more groups of words if at least one of the groups contains commas:

> Your supervisor, Mr. Smith, will be here Tuesday; Ms. Jones, his assistant, will be here Wednesday; and you, Bob, should be here every day.

> The hideous creature had fangs, tentacles, and a drooling maw; wings, claws, and piercing eyes; and blond, wavy hair.

COLONS

As with semi-colons, we use colons in only a few cases:

1. Use a colon after a complete sentence to introduce a list, a clause, or a quotation:

> Successful students have certain traits: patience, determination, ambition.

> Successful students have certain habits: they plan their work, they organize carefully, and they look for ways to improve their plans and organization.

> Steve quoted Mark Twain: "Perfect grammar—persistent, continuous, sustained—is the fourth dimension, so to speak; many have sought it, but none has found it."

Notice that in each example above, a word before the colon (traits, habits, quoted) announces or anticipates the words that follow it.

We are also allowed to place the list or phrase first, and then follow it with a colon and complete sentence:

Patience, determination, ambition: These are the qualities of a successful student.

In other words, a complete sentence must appear to the left or the right of a colon, or in both positions.

2. A colon never follows words like *include, such as,* or *like*:

WRONG: A successful student's qualities <u>include: patience</u>, determination, ambition.

RIGHT: A successful student's qualities <u>include patience</u>, determination, ambition.

WRONG: I want to take courses <u>such as: biology</u>, astronomy, and physics.

RIGHT: I want to take courses <u>such as biology</u>, astronomy, and physics.

3. A colon should appear at the end of a sentence that introduces a block quotation. (See the example in the section on ellipses and square brackets.)

4. When you introduce examples, with or without a colon, punctuate carefully. Both of these are correct:

He used many odd words (for example, *flabbergast, discombobulate,* and others).

He used many odd words: for example, *flabbergast, discombobulate,* and others.

If you wanted to use *e.g.* instead of *for example* in either of the sentences, the punctuation would not change:

He used many odd words (e.g., *flabbergast, discombobulate*, and others).

QUOTATION MARKS

It's easy for Americans to be confused about quotation marks because British books, periodicals, and websites use them differently. (The British are *wrong*, but don't tell them we said so.)

1. You never put quotation marks around the title of your own short story or essay, although you may put it in boldface type if you like. If you refer to your own work after it's published, *then* you include the quotation marks.

2. When referring to the short works of others (e.g., short stories and poems, articles, songs, or a web page within a larger site), enclose them in quotation marks: "The Raven," "The Star-Spangled Banner," "Frequently Asked Questions."

3. Titles of long works (books, newspapers, magazines, movies, plays, or entire websites) should be italicized: *The Lord of the Rings, The New York Times, The Best Years of Our Lives.*

    Before word processing and the personal computer, writers using typewriters <u>underlined</u> titles of long works—<u>The Lord of the Rings</u>—and some writers continue to do this. But now computers make italics so easy that we can leave this old-fashioned practice behind. Underlining is now usually reserved for graphic design purposes, as in some résumé formats.

    Many publications and websites still follow the old journalistic practice of enclosing titles of long works in quotation marks: "The Lord of the Rings." (In the long-ago past, when newspaper compositors set type by hand or with machines like Linotypes, switching from roman type to italics and back was uneconomically time-consuming.) If you're writing for one of those outlets, follow their rules.

4. Commas and periods always go to the immediate left of quotation marks—," ."—and never to the immediate right. Colons and semi-colons never go to the immediate left of the final quotation marks.

   Question marks and exclamation points go to the left only if they are part of the quotation or title:

   Louis Jordan wrote the song "Is You Is or Is You Ain't My Baby?"

   Didn't he also write "Baby, It's Cold Outside"?

   Notice that the first example above is a declarative sentence, but it has no period at the end. Only one final punctuation mark is required.

5. After an attribution of a quotation (e.g., *Paine wrote*), commas and quotation marks follow the verb (*wrote, stated, observed,* and others) unless one or more words follow the verb. Notice how the punctuation changes as the attribution or its placement changes:

   Thomas Paine wrote, "These are the times that try men's souls."

   Paine wrote that "These are the times that try men's souls."

   "These are the times," Paine wrote, "that try men's souls."

   "These are the times that try men's souls," as Thomas Paine wrote.

Did Paine write "These are the times that try men's souls"?

6. Single quotes are used inside double quotes. Commas and periods are placed inside single quotes:

Irving Berlin wrote "God Bless America."

The announcer said**,** "Irving Berlin wrote such popular songs as 'White Christmas,' 'There's No Business like Show Business,' and 'God Bless America.'"

Notice the three quotation marks after the period above.

See the example of block quotations in the section on ellipses and square brackets.

ELLIPSES AND SQUARE BRACKETS

We are permitted to delete words from direct quotations if we use ellipses (three spaced periods) to tell our readers (1) that words have been deleted and (2) where the deleted words were.

Similarly, we can add words to quotations by enclosing the additions in square brackets.

The following sentence, which contains a quotation, uses both ellipses and brackets:

In his book *The Great Movies*, film critic Roger Ebert writes that *The Maltese Falcon* is "[a]mong the movies we not only love but treasure. . . ."

In the original text by Ebert, the quoted words were at the beginning of a sentence, so the writer has used brackets to make the first letter of *among* lowercase. (The brackets for changing the capital are not always required, depending on the style guide you're using.)

Also notice that after the three ellipses, there is a fourth period to end the sentence.

Here's a second example, using a block quotation from Garry Wills's book *Certain Trumpets: The Nature of Leadership*. A block quotation is typically four or more lines long.

Here, the writer introduces the quotation from Wills with a complete sentence (*Wills explains* . . .) that ends in a colon. In the block quotation, the writer has deleted words with ellipses and inserted a comment in square brackets:

> Wills explains why radicals of the 1930's and 1940's objected to moderate leaders like Eleanor Roosevelt:
>
> > Those who reject the moderate leader because only a radical protest is "authentic" [a term describing protest that is believed to be sincere and effective] will never understand the need more ordinary people have for help to meet life's daily problems. Nor do they see how moderates alter power by making it more responsible . . . . Eleanor Roosevelt was "naïve" in the eyes of ideologues . . . who did not understand her extraordinary appeal.

As this example illustrates, block quotations have a wider left margin and are not enclosed in quotation marks. Within block quotations, use double quotations, as above.

ITALICS AND WRITING ABOUT LANGUAGE

When we write about words as words (i.e., as examples of language), those words should be *italicized*, although quotation marks are often used and are also correct.

When you speak of carrying something from one point to another, do you ever say *tote*, *lug*, or *schlep*?

You can use quotation marks in this sentence, but it complicates the punctuation:

Do you ever say "tote," "lug," or "schlep"?

PERIODS AND ABBREVIATIONS

It was long the rule to place a period after every initial letter in abbreviations like these: *U.S.A., U.K., U.N., N.A.S.A.*

Today in most (but not all) publications and contexts, we omit the periods: *USA, UK, UN, NASA* are now widely acceptable.

We still put periods after abbreviations that include the first letter and later letters in the same word: *Mr., Mrs., Ms., Dr., Sen.* (The British omit the periods in some of these, but we've already warned you about *them*.)

CAPITAL OFFENSES

You know most of the rules already, but here are a couple that may be new to you.

Capitalize *The* in the titles of books, newspapers, and other publications only if the word is part of the title. Thus we write *The New York Times,* but *the Chicago Tribune* and *the New York Daily News.*

In titles, it's usual to capitalize the first word, all nouns and verbs, and all adjectives and adverbs, but practices vary considerably. You'll have to consult the relevant style guide.

And do we write *earth* or *Earth*? Do we write *sun and moon*, or *Sun and Moon*? *Internet* or *internet*? Not even a dictionary can help with some words. Again, consult your style guide. Or make up your own mind and be consistent about it.

EXERCISES

21a. In the following sentences, place a comma wherever necessary.

1. Stephen Colbert the irreverent late-night host often pokes fun at political leaders.

2. Ralph Ellison's only completed novel Invisible Man won the National Book Award.

3. The rescue workers exhausted and discouraged stared at the rubble without speaking.

4. You can go when you are finished or you can stay and ask questions.

5. When you are finished you can go or you can stay and ask questions.

6. "He has plundered our seas ravaged our coasts burnt our towns and destroyed the lives of our people." (*The Declaration of Independence.*)

7. The long twisting and muddy road led to an abandoned car.

8. That movie which I've seen before is too violent for me.

9. He thought New York City New York was the greatest city on earth.

10. I have been working hard on my writing and I hope to do better in my next English class.

11. November 22 1963 is a day most Baby Boomers remember clearly.

21b. Which sentence below is unfair to teenaged drivers?

Restrictive: Teenaged drivers who drive like maniacs should lose their licenses.

Non-restrictive: Teenaged drivers, who drive like maniacs, should lose their licenses.

Which sentence below is unfair to grammarians?

Restrictive: Grammarians who are always correcting other people's grammar should be thrown out a second-story window.

Non-restrictive: Grammarians, who are always correcting other people's grammar, should be thrown out a second-story window.

21c. Insert a colon or semi-colon where necessary or correct a mistake.

1. He was fired yesterday he simply wasn't doing his job.

2. The boss offered only one explanation he simply wasn't doing his job.

3. A main clause contains a subject and a predicate it can stand alone as a complete sentence.

4. A main clause is easy to define it contains a subject and a predicate and can stand alone as a complete sentence.

5. Some interesting Southern expressions include: *tote, y'all,* and *schlimozel*.

6. *Tote, y'all,* and *schlimozel,* I'm not sure those are all Southern expressions.

21d. Correct punctuation as necessary in the following quotations. The first two are one sentence long; the third is two sentences.

1. My mother had a great deal of trouble with me wrote Mark Twain but I think she enjoyed it.

2. Elbert Hubbard wrote "Your friend is the man who knows all about you and still likes you.

3. [All of the following is a quotation from Jones, with a brief attribution in the middle of the quotation.]

   Senator Phogbound has an evasive word for everything Jones wrote. When he was caught tapping into his campaign funds, he called it "a possible error."

21e. Add or correct punctuation wherever necessary.

1. When theres a snow day we typically dont have to make it up unless weve had many of them.

2. Its always a relief after youve finished a research paper and turned it in.

3. St. Louis Missouri is Charles home and he returns there whenever he can

4. You can write one independent clause and its possible to add a second with a coordinating conjunction.

5. This is one independent clause this is another independent clause.

6. These are the steps in the writing process prewriting drafting revision and exhaustion.

7. Because its my grandmothers home Atlanta Georgia is my favorite city and Orlando Florida which is not that far from Atlanta is my favorite vacation spot.

8. My Aunt Hepatica still believes that Orson Welles drama the War of the Worlds was real. [Hint: It was a radio dramatization of a novel by H. G. Wells.]

Answer Key

CHAPTER 1

1a. The **simple subject** is the part of the sentence that names, without modifiers, who or what the sentence is about. The **simple predicate** is the part that says something about the subject. It also contains no modifiers or complements.

1b. Simple subject   Simple predicate
1. Rain   <u>falls</u>
2. Edward   <u>knocked</u>
3. family   <u>ate</u>
4. pancakes   <u>seemed</u>
5. Rudolpho   <u>rode</u>

1c. Simple subject   Simple predicate
1. Wendell   behaved
2. family   ate
3. sentences   ran
4. calla lilies   were
5. Rudolpho   was waiting

	Complete subject	Complete predicate
1.	Wendell	behaved politely
2.	that nice family	Tonight; ate on the porch again
3.	sentences	Backwards ran
4.	the calla lilies	In the spring; were in bloom again
5.	Rudolpho	This morning; was waiting on the porch for breakfast

CHAPTER 2

2a. In the sentences below, underline the complete predicates. Then enclose the simple subjects and simple predicates in brackets:

1. The [family] [was having] coffee.
2. The [family] [was] content.
3. Without warning, [John] [entered] the room.
4. [John] [made] an announcement.
5. The [vases] [are] gone.
6. The [family] [became] furious.
7. [Mr. Morton] [had struck] again.
8. [Mr. Morton] [had] some nerve.
9. Someday that [man] [will regret] his actions.
10. Mr. Morton's [reputation] [has been damaged] by these allegations.
11. Everywhere [people] [are hiding] their vases.
12. [Mr. Morton] [seems] a little strange.

2b. Now, in the sentences that you just examined, identify action verbs (with *A*) and linking verbs (with *L*):

1. A
2. L
3. A

4. A
5. L
6. L
7. A
8. A
9. A
10. A
11. A
12. L

2c. Finally, identify the auxiliary verbs and the main verb in each sentence you've examined. The main verbs are underlined.

1. was <u>having</u>
2. was
3. <u>entered</u>
4. <u>made</u>
5. <u>are</u>
6. <u>became</u>
7. had <u>struck</u>
8. <u>had</u>
9. will <u>regret</u>
10. has been <u>damaged</u>
11. are <u>hiding</u>
12. <u>seems</u>

CHAPTER 3

3a. Write from memory the simple and perfect tenses of the verb *call*.

SIMPLE PRESENT:	Today I call.
SIMPLE PAST:	Yesterday I called.
SIMPLE FUTURE:	Tomorrow I will call.

PRESENT PERFECT:	Today I have called.
PAST PERFECT:	As of yesterday, I had called.
FUTURE PERFECT:	By this time tomorrow, I will have called.

3b. Write from memory the simple progressive and perfect progressive tenses of the verb *call*.

PRESENT PROGRESSIVE:	Today I am calling.
PAST PROGRESSIVE:	Yesterday I was calling.
FUTURE PROGRESSIVE:	Tomorrow I will be calling.

PRESENT PERFECT PROGRESSIVE:	Today I have been calling.
PAST PERFECT PROGRESSIVE:	Yesterday I had been calling.
FUTURE PERFECT PROGRESSIVE:	Tomorrow I will have been calling.

3c. Write from memory the simple and perfect tenses of the verb *know*.

SIMPLE PRESENT:	Today I know.
SIMPLE PAST:	Yesterday I knew.
SIMPLE FUTURE:	Tomorrow I will know.

PRESENT PERFECT:	Today I have known.
PAST PERFECT:	As of yesterday, I had known.
FUTURE PERFECT:	By this time tomorrow, I will have known.

3d. Write from memory the simple progressive and perfect progressive tenses of the verb *know*.

PRESENT PROGRESSIVE:	Today I am knowing.
PAST PROGRESSIVE:	Yesterday I was knowing.
FUTURE PROGRESSIVE:	Tomorrow I will be knowing.

PRESENT PERFECT PROGRESSIVE: Today I have been knowing.
PAST PERFECT PROGRESSIVE: Yesterday I had been knowing.
FUTURE PERFECT PROGRESSIVE: Tomorrow I will have been knowing.

3e. Complete these sentences using the correct verb and the correct principal part:

1. I will **sit** here. (sit / set)
2. I will **set** my suitcase in the corner. (sit / set)

3. I will **raise** my bag to the top shelf. (rise / raise)
4. I will **rise** from my seat. (rise / raise)
5. I have **risen** from my seat. (risen / raised)
6. I have **raised** my bag. (risen / raised)

7. I will **lie** down. (lie / lay)
8. I will **lay** my bag over here. (lie / lay)
9. I have **lain** here for an hour. (lain / laid)
10. An hour ago, I **laid** my bag there. (lain / laid)

3f. Complete the sentences using one or more auxiliary verbs:

1. The perfect tenses use forms of the auxiliary verb **have.**
2. The progressive tenses use forms of the auxiliary verb **be.**
3. The perfect progressive tenses use forms of two auxiliary verbs: **have** and **be.**
4. All future tenses use the auxiliary **will.**

3g. Identify the tense of the verb in each of the following sentences using one of these twelve terms:

- Simple past, present, or future
- Present perfect, past perfect, or future perfect
- Present progressive, past progressive, or future progressive
- Present perfect progressive, past perfect progressive, or

future perfect progressive

1. She <u>was</u> here yesterday. **Simple past**
2. We <u>have been waiting</u> for you for an hour. **Present perfect progressive**
3. She <u>broke</u> her glasses. **Simple past**
4. She <u>has broken</u> her glasses twice. **Present perfect**
5. Yesterday's news <u>burst</u> all our illusions. **Simple past**
6. I <u>will speak</u> to the principal. **Simple future**
7. I <u>will be speaking</u> to the principal. **Future progressive**
8. We <u>had spoken</u> to the principal already. **Past perfect**
9. You <u>will have been speaking</u> to the principal for an hour. **Future perfect progressive**
10. I <u>have sung</u> this song before. **Present perfect**

3h. Complete the sentences using the names of principal parts of the verbs, or with the auxiliaries *will*, *have*, and *be*.

1. The perfect tenses are constructed using the third principal part, called the **past participle**.
2. The progressive tenses are constructed using the fourth principal part, called the **present participle**.
3. All future tense verbs begin with the auxiliary **will**.
4. All perfect tenses are constructed using some form of the auxiliary **have**.
5. All progressive tenses are constructed using some form of the auxiliary **be**.
6. The tenses constructed using both the auxiliaries *have* and *be* are called the **perfect progressive** tenses.

CHAPTER 4

4a. The three articles: *a, an, the*

4b. Identify the adjectives (including articles) in these sentences and underline them.

1. <u>The new</u> teacher is waiting in <u>the outer</u> office.
2. <u>A rainy</u> day could ruin <u>the entire</u> event.
3. Count Dracula is <u>the tall, pale</u> man <u>in the shadows</u>.
4. <u>A backyard</u> garden is <u>a wonderful</u> thing.
5. She wore <u>a red and white</u> dress to <u>the casual</u> party.
6. I gave <u>my little</u> brother <u>good</u> advice.
7. She has been <u>a better</u> student <u>this</u> year because of <u>her hard</u> work.
8. <u>Bob's</u> idea is <u>the worst</u> idea I've heard in <u>a long</u> time.
9. <u>The point-by-point</u> refutation was <u>a difficult</u> argument to follow.
10. <u>Two</u> roads lead to <u>his</u> farm.
11. <u>Which</u> roads are those?

4c. Give the comparative and superlative forms of these adjectives; use a dictionary when you need to. In some cases, there may be no comparative or superlative forms.

1. Small, smaller, smallest
2. Fast, faster, fastest
3. Bright, brighter, brightest
4. Good, better, best
5. Bad, worse, worst
6. Curious, more curious, most curious
7. Cheerful, more cheerful, most cheerful
8. Happy, happier, happiest
9. Wrong: There are no comparative or superlative forms for *wrong*.
10. Far, further, furthest

CHAPTER 5

5a. In the following sentences, mark the underlined words to classify them as adjectives (*ADJ*) or adverbs (*ADV*). Count the articles *a, an,* and *the* as adjectives. The adverbs here modify verbs only.

      ADJ ADJ   ADJ ADJ
1. The smaller child learned the simplest tasks.

     ADJ   ADV
2. The child learns eagerly.

        ADV   ADJ   ADJ ADJ
3. John almost had an answer to the difficult question.

         ADV   ADJ
4. Father always encourages realistic thinking.

     ADJ ADJ   ADV   ADJ ADJ
5. The furious family did not wait to see the busy manager.

     ADJ ADJ ADJ   ADV
6. A thick, wet snow fell softly.

     ADV   ADJ ADJ   ADJ ADJ   ADJ
7. Silently, a strange man in a black cape stood in the shadows.

5b. Write the comparative and superlative forms of these adverbs; use a dictionary when you need to.

1. Fast, faster, fastest
2. Quickly, more quickly, most quickly
3. Slowly, more slowly, most slowly
4. Angrily, more angrily, most angrily
5. Carefully, more carefully, most carefully
6. Well, better, best
7. Badly, worse, worst
8. Early, earlier, earliest
9. Far, farther, farthest
10. Often, more often, most often

5c. In these sentences, classify the underlined adverbs: Do they modify verbs, adjectives, or other adverbs?

1. Your mistake was a <u>very</u> small one. (Modifies the adjective *small*.)
2. He does <u>well</u> when he tries <u>hard</u>. (*Well* modifies the verbs *does*; *hard* modifies *tries*.)
3. He does <u>quite</u> well when he tries. (Modifies the adverb *well*.)
4. The secretary's notes are <u>evidently</u> missing. (Modifies the verb *missing*.)
5. <u>Now</u> we <u>finally</u> have the notes. (Both *now* and *finally* modify the verb *have*.)
6. We took notes <u>rather</u> <u>rapidly</u>, but we could <u>not</u> keep up. (*Rather* modifies the adverb *rapidly*; *rapidly* modifies the verb *took*; *not* modifies the verb *keep up*.)
7. We <u>still</u> need good notes. (Modifies the verb *need*.)

5d. The underlined adjectives and adverbs have been corrected:

1. Esther and Ryan play <u>well</u>, but Esther plays <u>better</u>.
2. By sunset we will have hiked ten miles or <u>farther</u>.
3. The library has the <u>most complete book</u> on baseball.
4. Bob was the <u>only</u> student left behind.
5. <u>Finally</u> we reached the motel.

6. Be _really_ careful on this highway.
7. We saw that Bart looked _sad_.
8. Bart was looking _sadly_ at his wrecked car.
9. Bart was feeling _sad_ on his way home.
10. In the lab, we measured the results as _precisely_ as we could.

CHAPTER 6

6a. In the following sentences <u>underline</u> the prepositional phrases and <u>double-underline</u> the preposition. Some sentences contain more than one prepositional phrase. If you need to, refer to the lists of prepositions in this chapter.

1. <u>In the morning</u>, I drink coffee <u>with cream</u>.
2. <u>As a rule</u>, I never put sugar <u>in it</u>.
3. <u>Amid cars and trucks</u>, Edwina ran <u>across the street</u>.
4. I am looking <u>for the owner</u> <u>of this dog</u>.
5. Are you referring <u>to the dog</u> that is nipping <u>at your leg</u>?
6. <u>Throughout the book</u>, the author emphasizes the influence <u>of history</u> <u>upon our perception</u> <u>of events</u>.
7. <u>Like Arthur</u>, I walked <u>down the hall</u> and paid no attention <u>to the noise</u> <u>within the office</u>.
8. <u>According to Arthur</u>, the noise <u>out of the office</u> was <u>because of an argument</u> <u>between Ed and Grace</u>.
9. Arthur should not have been left <u>in charge</u> <u>of the office</u> <u>during the summer</u>.
10. <u>In case</u> <u>of further conflicts</u>, we should make plans <u>regarding appropriate training</u> <u>for all employees</u>.

6b. After you finish Exercise 6a, go back through the ten sentences above and decide if the prepositional phrases are adjectival (ADJ) or adverbial (ADV), and label them accordingly.

1. <u>In the morning</u> [ADV], I drink coffee <u>with cream</u> [ADJ].

2. <u>As a rule</u> [ADV], I never put sugar <u>in it</u> [ADV].

3. <u>Amid cars and trucks</u> [ADV], Edwina ran <u>across the street</u> [ADV].

4. I am looking <u>for the owner</u> [ADV] <u>of this dog</u> [ADJ].

5. Are you referring <u>to the dog</u> [ADV] that is nipping <u>at your leg</u> [ADV]?

6. <u>Throughout the book</u> [ADV], the author emphasizes the influence <u>of history</u> [ADJ] <u>upon our perception</u> [ADJ] <u>of events</u> [ADJ].

7. <u>Like Arthur</u> [ADV], I walked <u>down the hall</u> [ADV] and paid no attention <u>to the noise</u> [ADJ] <u>within the office</u> [ADJ].

8. <u>According to Arthur</u> [ADV], the noise <u>out of the office</u> [ADJ] was

     ADV   ADJ
  because of an argument between Ed and Grace.

            ADV ADJ
9. Arthur should not have been left in charge of the office
    ADV
  during the summer.

   ADV   ADJ
10. In case of further conflicts, we should make plans
     ADJ   ADJ
  regarding appropriate training for all employees.

CHAPTER 7

7a. In this exercise, you need to write five versions of the same short sentence. Each version will use a different pronoun.

 First read the pronouns in the parentheses after each sentence. Then, for each pronoun, find the correct case to insert into the blank. Consult the pronoun tables in this chapter if you need to.

 The answers are italicized:

1. You can go with _____. (I, he, we, they, she): *me, him, us, them, her*
2. We will take _____ to the mall. (he, she, they, you): *him, her, them, you*
3. _____ can go with me. (him, her, you, them, us): *He, She, You, They, We*
4. That isn't your book. It's _____. (I, he, we, they, she): *mine, his, ours, theirs, hers*
5. We won't go to your place. We'll go to _____ place. (I, he, we, they, she): *my, his, our, their, her*

7b. Write the pronoun that is specified by the terms. Usually only one pronoun is possible for each exercise. Consult the pronoun tables when you need to.

1. First-person objective singular: *me*
2. First-person objective plural: *us*
3. Second-person nominative singular (or plural): *you*
4. Feminine third-person nominative singular: *she*
5. Third-person nominative plural: *they*
6. Third-person objective singular: *him, her,* or *it*
7. Third-person objective plural: *them*
8. First-person nominative plural: *we*
9. First-person possessive singular: *my* or *mine*
10. Neuter third-person nominative singular: *it*

7c. Classify the following pronouns according to person, case, and number. With the third-person singular pronouns, also classify gender (masculine, feminine, or neuter). Consult the tables when necessary.

1. My (First-person possessive singular)
2. He (Third-person nominative masculine singular)
3. Him (Third-person objective masculine singular)
4. Its (Third-person possessive neuter singular)
5. Yours (Second-person possessive singular or plural)
6. We (First-person nominative plural)
7. Us (First-person objective plural)
8. Our (First-person possessive plural)
9. They (Third-person nominative plural)
10. Them (Third-person objective plural)

7d. In the following sentences, identify and correct carelessly used pronouns. In the answers below, corrected words are underlined, and correct sentences are unchanged.

1. If anyone sees a problem, <u>please</u> report it immediately.
2. Neither excessive heat nor cold will damage the crop unless <u>the extreme weather</u> lasts for weeks.
3. <u>It's</u> time to study grammar.
4. If <u>you</u> want to do well in this course, <u>you</u> should be prepared to work hard.
5. Each of these books has <u>its</u> correct place on the shelves.
6. <u>Jerry was helped to his apartment by Jim</u>.
7. Medical <u>doctors</u> <u>need</u> to know <u>their</u> science well.
8. Our dog has something in <u>its</u> paw.
9. The <u>car</u> needs a new transmission, and the tires need replacing, but I only paid five hundred dollars for <u>it</u>.
10. As the bicyclists sped by the crowd, some <u>bikers</u> nearly hit <u>onlookers</u>.

7e. Complete the following tables for the simple tenses of the verb *to be*.

Simple tenses:

Singular	Present	Past	Future
1st person	I am	I was	I will be
2nd person	You are	You were	You will be
3rd person	He is	He was	He will be

Plural	Present	Past	Future
1st person	We are	We were	We will be
2nd person	You are	You were	You will be
3rd person	They are	They were	They will be

7f. Complete the following table for the perfect tenses of the verb *to be*. Also provide pronouns as subjects of the verbs.

Singular	Present	Past	Future
1st person	I have been	I had been	I will have been
2nd person	You have been	You had been	You will have been
3rd person	He has been	He had been	He will have been

7g. Complete the following tables for the progressive and perfect progressive tenses of the verb *to be*. Also provide pronouns as subjects of the verbs.

Progressive

Singular	Present	Past	Future
1st person	I am being	I was being	I will be being
2nd person	You are being	You were being	You will be being
3rd person	She is being	She was being	She will be being

Perfect Progressive

Singular	Present	Past	Future
1st person	I have been being	I had been being	I will have been being
2nd person	You have been being	You had been being	You will have been being
3rd person	She has been being	She had been being	She will have been being

CHAPTER 8

8a. In the following sentences, fill in the blanks with one word: *always, never,* or *sometimes*.

1. Sentences with action verbs _sometimes_ have a complement.
2. Sentences with linking verbs _always_ have a complement.
3. Sentences with intransitive verbs _never_ have a complement.
4. Sentences with transitive verbs _always_ have a complement.
5. Sentences with transitive verbs _always_ have a direct object.
6. Sentences with transitive verbs _sometimes_ have an indirect object.
7. Sentences with linking verbs _sometimes_ have a predicate nominative.
8. Sentences with transitive verbs _never_ have a predicate adjective.
9. Sentences with linking verbs _sometimes_ have a predicate adjective.
10. Sentences with transitive verbs _sometimes_ have an object complement.
11. Sentences with linking verbs _never_ have an object complement.
12. Sentences with linking verbs _never_ have a direct object.

8b. In the sentences below, identify the complements and classify them as a direct object, an indirect object, a predicate adjective, a predicate nominative, or an object complement.

1. My daughter made me proud. *Direct object, object complement*
2. My aunt brought me a souvenir. *Indirect object, direct object*
3. My sister is late. *Predicate adjective*
4. Both my sisters are teachers. *Predicate nominative*
5. Both my sisters are arriving at noon. *No complement*
6. Six hours a day, Ruthie practices the accordion. *Direct object*
7. Ruthie practices for hours every day. *No complement*
8. We sent Bill and Sue a gift. *Indirect object, direct object*
9. They were kind and grateful. *Compound predicate adjective*
10. I will address that issue at another time. *Direct object*

11. That fellow became <u>our assistant</u>. *Predicate nominative*
12. Bonnie bought <u>Ed</u> <u>that painting</u>. *Indirect object, direct object*

8c. Now go back through the sentences above and identify the verbs as linking, transitive, or intransitive.

1. My daughter <u>made</u> me proud. *Transitive*
2. My aunt <u>brought</u> me a souvenir. *Transitive*
3. My sister <u>is</u> late. *Linking*
4. Both my sisters <u>are</u> teachers. *Linking*
5. Both my sisters <u>are arriving</u> at noon *Intransitive*
6. Six hours a day, Ruthie <u>practices</u> the accordion. *Transitive*
7. Ruthie <u>practices</u> for hours every day. *Intransitive*
8. We <u>sent</u> Bill and Sue a gift. *Transitive*
9. They <u>were</u> kind and grateful. *Linking*
10. I <u>will address</u> that issue at another time. *Transitive*
11. That fellow <u>became</u> our assistant. *Linking*
12. Bonnie <u>bought</u> Ed that painting. *Transitive*

CHAPTER 9

9a. Try to write, from memory, the seven coordinating conjunctions. (A hint: Remember *FANBOYS*.) Check your answers with the list in this chapter.

for, and, nor, but, or, yet, so

9b. Try to write, from memory, the four correlative coordinating conjunctions. Check your answers with the list in this chapter.

Either . . . or; neither . . . nor; not only . . . but also; both . . . and

9c. Try to write, from memory, ten of the subordinating conjunctions, and consult the chapter to check your answers.

after	once	when
although	since	whenever
as	than	where
because	that	wherever
before	though	whereas
however	till	whether
if	unless	while
lest	until	

9d. In the following sentences, underline and classify the conjunctions as coordinating (C) or subordinating (S) and put brackets around any prepositions. Refer to the lists in this chapter and the previous chapter if you need to. Classify correlative conjunctions as coordinating.

Here's an example:

                              C
[In] the following sentences, underline <u>and</u> classify the conjunctions
        C   C
[as] coordinating <u>or</u> subordinating <u>and</u> put brackets [around] any prepositions.

                          C   C   C
1.   The film was <u>not only</u> boring, <u>but also</u> offensive, <u>so</u> we asked
        C
[for] a refund <u>and</u> went home.

                    C
2.   [In] the morning <u>and</u> again [in] the evening, Ruthie
                        S
practices her violin <u>until</u> her mother can't stand it anymore.

3. We went [to] the diner [for] lunch, <u>for</u> we were expected back soon. (C above "for")

4. <u>Because</u> we are tired, we'll take a short break <u>before</u> we continue studying. (S, S)

5. Fred <u>and</u> George have been gone [since] Friday night, <u>since</u> they took a "short break" [from] studying. (C, S)

6. <u>After</u> I finish this project, we can meet [after] work <u>and</u> discuss the project. (S, C)

7. Frank <u>and</u> George are <u>neither</u> punctual <u>nor</u> organized, <u>yet</u> they somehow do their work well. (C, C, C, C)

8. He was <u>so</u> confident <u>that</u> he underestimated his opponent. (S, S)

9. The room looked <u>as if</u> it had not been occupied [in] some time, <u>but</u> it had been occupied [for] days <u>or</u> weeks. (S; C, C)

No conjunctions

10. <u>The</u> longer he waited, <u>the</u> more impatient he became.

9e. In the following sentences, identify and label compound subjects, compound verbs, compound predicates, and other compound structures, but not clauses.

1. Anne always <u>fastens her seatbelt and locks her doors</u> before she drives. *Compound predicate*
2. <u>Anne and James</u> are driving to <u>Nashville and Chattanooga</u>. *Compound subject and compound object of the preposition*
3. In Nashville, Anne <u>shopped and visited her family</u>. *Compound predicate*
4. <u>She and I</u> <u>always enjoy Nashville, but seldom get to go there</u>. *Compound subject and compound predicate*
5. The next day we will drive from Tennessee to Illinois. *No compounds here*
6. In Illinois, we will visit <u>the Lincoln Museum and the Lincoln Library</u>. *Compound direct object.*
7. We will stop <u>in Wisconsin or Minnesota</u> for the night. *Compound object of the preposition* in.
8. In Minnesota we <u>will ski and visit family</u>. *Compound predicate.*
9. <u>Anne and her sister Alice</u> love skiing. *Compound subject.*
10. In cold weather, James <u>stays indoors and reads</u>. *Compound predicate.*

CHAPTER 10

10a. Go back to the beginning pages of this chapter and reread the definitions of an independent clause, a dependent clause, and a sentence. Then try to write the three definitions from memory, and use the book to check your work.

An independent clause contains at least one subject and at least one predicate, and it contains no word (like a subordinating conjunction or a relative pronoun) that makes the clause dependent on another clause to be complete.

A dependent clause contains at least one subject and at least one predicate, and it is not grammatically complete by itself.

A sentence is a unit of language that contains at least one independent clause. It may also contain one or more dependent clauses.

10b. Classify the following sentences according to their structures. Each sentence will be simple, compound, complex, or compound-complex. Refer to the definitions in this chapter when you need to.

1. My family owned a cocker spaniel when I was young. *Complex*
2. Before the meeting, we will set up the room, and you should prepare the refreshments. *Compound*
3. Before the meeting begins, we will set up the room, and you should prepare the refreshments. *Compound-complex*
4. He has done well since graduation, and he credits his success to the university. *Compound*
5. As if he is the supervisor. *Fragment*
6. Since graduation, when he began working here, while Arthur was the supervisor of both departments. *Fragment*
7. Louise and Sharon went to the garage and found their car. *Simple*
8. Either Arthur and Gwyn find a way to solve this problem themselves, or they must seek help. *Compound*
9. Both spring and fall are their favorite seasons for camping and fishing in the mountains. *Simple*
10. We sat nervously as we waited for our interviews. *Complex*

11. During our interviews, the applicants occasionally answered poorly, but in general they did well. *Compound*
12. After they left the office, they returned, for Louise had forgotten her portfolio. *Compound-complex*

10c. Return to the sentences in **10b**, and identify the complete subjects and predicates in all the clauses of all the complete sentences. Put subjects in brackets and underline predicates.

1. [My family] <u>owned a cocker spaniel</u> when [I] <u>was young</u>.
2. <u>Before the meeting</u>, [we] <u>will set up the room</u>, and [you] <u>should prepare the refreshments</u>.
3. Before [the meeting] <u>begins</u>, [we] <u>will set up the room</u>, and [you] <u>should prepare the refreshments</u>.
4. [He] <u>has done well since graduation</u>, and [he] <u>credits his success to the university</u>.
5. *This is a fragment sentence.*
6. *This is also a fragment sentence.*
7. [Louise and Sharon] <u>went to the garage and found their car</u>.
8. Either [Arthur and Gwyn] <u>find a way to solve this problem themselves,</u> or [they] <u>must seek help</u>.
9. [Both spring and fall] <u>are their favorite seasons for camping in the mountains and fishing</u>.
10. [We] <u>sat nervously</u> as [we] <u>waited for our interviews</u>.
11. <u>During the interviews</u>, [the applicants] <u>occasionally answered poorly</u>, but<u> in general</u> [they]<u> did well</u>.
12. After [they] <u>left the office</u>, [they] <u>returned</u>, for [Louise] <u>had forgotten her portfolio</u>.

10d. Classify the following sentences according to their purposes: Each sentence will be declarative, interrogative, imperative, or exclamatory. (Don't worry about possible implicit meanings.) Refer to the definitions in this chapter when you need to.

1. What a mess! *Exclamatory*
2. What are you shouting about? *Interrogative*
3. I forgot my portfolio, and now the office is closed. *Declarative*
4. Just relax and get it tomorrow. *Imperative*
5. Listen! *Imperative*
6. The boys' choir is singing. *Imperative*
7. What music those children make! *Exclamatory*
8. Didn't Count Dracula say that once? *Interrogative*
9. Are you comparing the boys' choir to wolves? *Interrogative*
10. Stop twisting my words! *Imperative*

CHAPTER 11

11a. Underline the relative clauses in the following sentences. Double-underline the relative pronouns. Locate the nouns modified by each relative clause and enclose them in square brackets. Remember that some uses of *that* are not relative pronouns. You'll see an example here.

1. The [house] <u>that is being renovated</u> was my grandmother's home.
2. Please get the [book], <u>which I left in my office</u>.
3. You can give that letter to the [man] <u>who is waiting outside</u>.
4. The [woman] <u>whose car you dented</u> wants to speak to you.
5. The [man] <u>who is waiting</u> already has that letter <u>that you left in your office.</u>
6. The [customer] <u>whom you phoned</u> is waiting in the office.
7. I know the [man] <u>to whom they spoke</u>.

11b. Underline the relative clauses in the following sentences. Double-underline the relative adverbs. Locate the nouns modified by each relative clause and enclose them in square brackets.

1. The [house] <u>where he was born</u> is on Fifth Street.

2. In [April 1943], <u>when he was born</u>, his parents were living and working in the city.
3. Spring is the [season] <u>when I am happiest</u>, and home is the [place] <u>where all of us are most comfortable</u>.
4. [Marceline], <u>where Walt Disney grew up</u>, is a small town in northern Missouri.
5. In [1911], <u>when his family moved to Kansas City</u>, Disney left Marceline.

11c. Rewrite each of the following pairs of sentences as a single sentence with a relative clause. Make the second sentence the relative clause. <u>Underline</u> the relative clause in each new sentence.

A reminder: The relative pronouns are *who, whom, whose, which,* and *that*.

1. That man <u>who is standing over there</u> is my neighbor.
2. I like the car <u>that you rented today</u>.
3. The woman <u>whom you called earlier</u> is at the door.
4. The dog <u>that I lost has</u> been found.
5. My mother, <u>who loves old movies</u>, is watching *Casablanca*.

11d. Rewrite each pair of sentences as one sentence with a relative clause. Make the second sentence the relative clause. <u>Underline</u> the relative clause in each new sentence.

1. Gary, Indiana, <u>where I was born</u>, is a pleasant small city.
2. I walked down the street <u>where she lives</u>.
3. Christmas is a wonderful time of year <u>when my entire family gathers together</u>.
4. There is the hospital <u>where I was born</u>.
5. The book is in the living room <u>where Ron is reading</u>.

CHAPTER 12

12a. In the following sentences, identify the functions of each underlined nominal clause.

1. I know <u>why you did that</u>. *Direct object*
2. I can't imagine <u>what they will do next</u> or <u>who will do it</u>. *Compound direct object*
3. <u>When they arrive</u> is unknown. *Subject*
4. You already know <u>that they don't know the area well</u>. *Direct object*
5. <u>Why they come here</u> is a mystery. *Subject*
6. The professor is writing a book about <u>how people improve their writing</u>. *Object of a preposition*
7. <u>Whether he will succeed</u> is <u>what we are all wondering</u>. *Subject and predicate nominative*
8. He discussed why climate change is happening. *Direct object*
9. When he arrives, I will tell him <u>when we are leaving</u>. *Direct object*

12b. In the following sentences, underline the nominal clauses and then identify their functions in each sentence.

1. The statement summarizes <u>what he is saying</u>. *Direct object*
2. We will learn <u>if tickets are still available</u>. *Direct object*
3. <u>When we will meet</u> is the next topic. *Subject*
4. I have a question about <u>who broke the equipment</u>. *Object of the preposition*
5. I will tell <u>whoever is interested</u> about the news. *Direct object*
6. I don't know <u>why he left</u>. *Direct object*
7. His claim was <u>that he was abducted by aliens</u>. *Predicate nominative* His wife made him <u>what he is today</u>. *Object complement* I don't think <u>that we should blame that on his wife</u>. *Direct object*

8. We were taught <u>that anything that is worth doing is worth doing well</u>. [This is complicated: The underlined clause is a *Direct object*. But the shorter clause *that is worth doing* is a relative clause modifying *anything*.]

CHAPTER 13

13a. In the following sentences, classify the underlined dependent clauses as either subordinate or nominal.

1. I will see <u>if we have any milk</u>. *Nominal*
2. I will go to the store <u>if we are out of milk</u>. *Subordinate*
3. <u>Whether or not we are out of milk</u>, I will go to the store. *Subordinate*
4. I wonder <u>whether we are out of milk</u>. *Nominal*
5. I go to the store <u>when we are out of milk</u>. *Subordinate*
6. I will know <u>whether we are out of milk</u>. *Nominal*
7. I can't understand <u>how we could be out of milk</u>. *Nominal*
8. I don't know <u>why we are out of milk</u>. *Nominal*
9. <u>Why we are out of milk</u> is <u>what I want to know</u>. *Nominal*
10. I told you <u>that we would run out of milk</u>. *Nominal*

13b. In this next set, identify the dependent clauses and classify them as either subordinate or nominal.

1. Go see <u>if Jim is here</u>. *Nominal*
2. We will start dinner <u>if Jim is here</u>. *Subordinate*
3. <u>If Jim is here</u>, we can have dinner. *Subordinate*
4. <u>If Jim is here</u> is <u>what I want to know</u>. *Two nominals*
5. I need to know <u>whether Jim has arrived</u>. *Nominal*
6. <u>Whether or not he has arrived</u>, we will now have dinner. *Subordinate*
7. <u>When Jim arrives</u>, we will have dinner. *Subordinate*
8. I know <u>when Jim will arrive</u>. *Nominal.*

9. Please tell me <u>how we can have dinner</u> <u>if Jim is not here</u>. *Nominal and subordinate*

13c. Classify the underlined dependent clauses as either *relative* (adjectival) clauses or as *nominal* clauses:

1. I know <u>that she likes me</u>. *Nominal*
2. <u>That she likes me</u> surprises me. *Nominal*
3. That is the class <u>that I want</u>. *Relative*
4. That is the class <u>that challenges me</u>. *Relative*
5. The people <u>who like me</u> are over there. *Relative*
6. I know <u>who likes you</u>. *Nominal*
7. <u>What fascinates me</u> is calculus. *Nominal*
8. We'll learn <u>why spring begins</u>. *Nominal*
9. The day <u>when spring begins</u> is next week. *Relative*
10. I know the place <u>where I can enroll</u>. *Relative*

13d. Identify the dependent clauses in these sentences and classify them as *relative* (adjectival) clauses or *nominal* clauses:

1. I know <u>who that is</u>. *Nominal*
2. I will take the book <u>that is least expensive</u>. *Relative*
3. There is the fellow <u>whom I've met before</u>. *Relative*
4. I know <u>whom you spoke with</u>. *Nominal*
5. There is the woman <u>who hired me</u>. *Relative*
6. The dog <u>that bit me</u> is in that yard. *Relative*
7. <u>Who steals my purse</u> steals my gum. *Nominal*
8. I have learned <u>what the answer is</u>. *Nominal*

13e. Identify the dependent clauses in the following sentences and classify them as *relative* or as *subordinate*. Some sentences have two dependent clauses:

1. <u>Because it is late</u>, we will wait until tomorrow to see the movie <u>that you want to see</u>. *Subordinate, Relative*

2. <u>When we saw *The Martian*</u>, we enjoyed the story about the space traveler <u>who is marooned alone on a planet</u>. *Subordinate, Relative*
3. We were quite surprised by the film <u>that we saw last night</u> *Relative*
4. This is the theatre <u>where we saw that film</u>. *Relative*
5. Is this the time <u>when the next film is shown</u>? *Relative*
6. You should tell your friends <u>when you see a good film</u>. *Subordinate*
7. <u>Where I come from</u>, we have several good movie theatres. *Subordinate*

13f. Finally, here's an exercise that will help you bring together all the concepts in this chapter. Identify the dependent clauses in the following sentences and classify them as *relative*, as *subordinate*, or as *nominal* clauses:

1. The place <u>that we call home</u> is Peoria. *Relative*
2. I must see <u>if they are here</u>. *Nominal*
3. I know <u>that they have arrived</u>. *Nominal*
4. I read an article about the accident <u>that we saw yesterday</u>. *Relative*
5. We will see <u>if the storm will hit</u>. *Nominal*
6. <u>If the storm hits</u>, we will be ready. *Subordinate*
7. I know the time <u>when they will arrive</u>. *Relative*
8. The town <u>where I was born</u> is very small. *Relative*
9. I wonder <u>where he was born</u>. *Nominal*
10. I will go to the airport <u>when he arrives</u>. *Subordinate*
11. <u>Whether we want to go or not</u>, we must be at the airport. *Subordinate*
12. I do not know <u>whether he will be on the plane</u>. *Nominal*

CHAPTER 14

14a. Rewrite the following passive-voice sentences as active-voice sentences, as in this example:

PASSIVE: I was given a prescription by my doctor.
ACTIVE: My doctor gave me a prescription last night.

1. Your letter was received by me.
   ACTIVE: I received your letter.

2. I was made happy by your letter.
   ACTIVE: Your letter made me happy.

3. I was given instructions today by my supervisor.
   ACTIVE: My supervisor gave me instructions today.

4. My last essay was given a C by my English teacher.
   ACTIVE: My English teacher gave my last essay a C.

5. I was seen at the mall by Cheryl.
   ACTIVE: Cheryl saw me at the mall.

6. The mail was delivered by the postman at noon.
   ACTIVE: The postman delivered the mail at noon.

7. After the symphony was played beautifully by the orchestra, the composer was praised by the critics.
   ACTIVE: After the orchestra played the symphony beautifully, the critics praised the composer.

14b. In the passive sentences above, locate, underline, and identify the passive complements: the direct object (DO), the predicate adjective (PA), and the predicate nominate (PN), as in this example:

                                DO
PASSIVE: I was given <u>a prescription</u> by my doctor last night.

    No complement
1. Your letter was received by me.

                                PA
2. I was made <u>happy</u> by your letter.

                                DO
3. I was given <u>instructions</u> today by my supervisor.

                                DO
4. My last essay was given a <u>C</u> by my English teacher.

    No complement
5. I was seen at the mall by Cheryl.

    No complement
6. The mail was delivered by the postman at noon.

    No complement
7. After the symphony was played beautifully by the orchestra, the composer was praised by the critics.

14c. Distinguish phrasal verbs from verbs followed by prepositional phrases, as in these examples:

    I'll <u>turn on</u> the television.
    [Phrasal verb]

That new car can turn <u>on a dime</u>.
[Verb and prepositional phrase]

1. We'll turn <u>off the highway</u> at the next exit. [Verb and prepositional phrase]

   Please <u>turn off</u> the radio. [Phrasal verb]

2. The news <u>comes on</u> at 10 pm. [Phrasal verb]
   The gifts came <u>on Christmas Eve</u>. [Verb and prepositional phrase]

3. The pumpkin <u>turned into</u> a beautiful coach. [Phrasal verb]
   We'll turn <u>into this driveway</u>. [Verb and prepositional phrase]

4. They took the dresser <u>up the stairs</u>. [Verb and prepositional phrase]
   We will now <u>take up</u> the collection. [Phrasal verb]

5. He <u>called out</u> to her before she drove away. [Phrasal verb]
   He called <u>out the window</u>. [Verb and prepositional phrase]

CHAPTER 15

15a. What's the difference <u>in writing</u> between regular plural nouns, possessive nouns, and plural possessive nouns? Write an example that illustrates each category, using words that have regular plurals.

For example: *cats, cat's,* and *cats'*.

Regular plurals take only –s, possessives take an apostrophe followed by –s, and plural possessives take –s, followed by an apostrophe.

15b. Write plural, singular possessive, and plural possessive forms of the following nouns: *woman, ox, church, tomato, piano, medium* (e.g., *the medium of TV*), *boss,* and *octopus.*

Singular	Plural	Singular Possessive	Plural Possessive
woman	women	woman's	women's
ox	oxen	ox's	oxen's
church	churches	church's	churches'
tomato	tomatoes	tomato's	tomatoes'
piano	pianos	piano's	pianos'
medium	media	medium's	media's
boss	bosses	boss's	bosses'
octopus	octopi	octopus's	octopi's

15c. In the following sentences, identify the sentences that contain nouns of address, appositives, and expletives, and underline those structures. In sentences with expletives, identify the subject of the sentence. A sentence may contain more than one of these structures. In some cases, the function of the phrase may not be clear within the limited context.

1. Dr. Kildare, you can speak with my assistant. [Noun of address]
2. June, speak with my physician, Dr. Kildare. [Noun of address and appositive]
3. Your brother, Alice, is remarkable. [Noun of address, unless *Alice* is your brother's name]
4. There is rain forecast for tomorrow. [Expletive, and *rain* is the subject]
5. It is clear that Ed is a menace. [Expletive: The nominal clause *that Ed is a menace* is the subject.]

CHAPTER 16

16a. Write from memory the eight parts of speech. Then define them and check your work by referring to the early pages of this chapter.

Nouns: Words that stand for persons, places, things, or ideas.

Pronouns: Words that take the place of nouns.

Adjectives: Words that modify nouns or pronouns.

Verbs: Words that indicate an action or a state of being.

Adverbs: Words that modify verbs, adjectives, or other adverbs.

Conjunctions: Words that connect phrases and clauses to other phrases or clauses, indicating some grammatical relationship between the connected units.

Prepositions: Words that connect a noun or pronoun (the object of the preposition) with other words in the sentence to create adjectival or adverbial phrases.

Interjections: Exclamatory words and phrases used to express feelings and reactions.

16b. In the following sentences, use context to identify the form and function of the underlined words.

1. In the increasingly chaotic country, university students are <u>revolting</u>.
   Form: A verb (present participle).
   Function: The main verb.

2. Defend them if you like, but I'm tired of these <u>revolting</u> students.
   Form: A verb (present participle).
   Function: Adjectival, modifying *students*.

3. We were <u>jogging</u> around the block.
   Form: A verb (present participle).
   Function: The main verb.

4. All of us enjoy <u>jogging</u>.
   Form: A verb (present participle).
   Function: Nominal, as the direct object of *enjoy*.

5. He will replace the <u>shattered</u> lamp.
   Form: A verb (past participle).
   Function: Adjectival, modifying *lamp*.

6. He <u>shattered</u> it accidentally.
   Form: A verb (past participle).
   Function: The main verb.

7. This rose bud is <u>for</u> you.
   Form: A preposition.
   Function: Part of the adverbial prepositional phrase *for you*.

8. I gave you a rose bud, <u>for</u> I care about you.
   Form: A coordinating conjunction.
   Function: Joining two independent clauses.

9. I wanted to get you more, <u>but</u> I couldn't afford it.
   Form: A coordinating conjunction.
   Function: Joining two independent clauses.

10. I bought you nothing <u>but</u> this rose bud.
    Form: A preposition, synonymous with *except*.
    Function: Part of the adjectival prepositional phrase *but this rose bud*.

CHAPTER 17

17a. Identify the functions of the underlined gerunds in these sentences:

1. <u>Farming</u> is his business. *Subject*
2. His business is <u>farming</u>. *Predicate nominative*
3. He likes <u>farming</u>. *Direct object*
4. He likes <u>raising corn and soy beans</u>. *Compound direct object*
5. He will stay with <u>farming</u>. *Object of the preposition*
6. His profession, <u>raising corn and soy beans</u>, is a difficult one. *A compound appositive*

17b. Now locate the gerunds in the following and identify their functions.

[In these answers the gerund phrases, with modifiers and complements, are underlined.]

1. His hobby is <u>biking</u>. *Predicate nominative*
2. <u>Biking</u> is his hobby. *Subject*
3. He is interested in <u>biking</u>. *Object of a preposition*
4. His hobby, <u>biking</u>, is a popular one. *Appositive*
5. <u>Biking ten miles a day</u> is a challenge. *Subject*
6. His goal is <u>biking ten miles a day</u>. *Predicate nominative*
7. He makes time for <u>biking ten miles a day</u>. *Object of a preposition*
8. She likes <u>being a patrol officer</u>. *Direct object*
9. <u>Being a patrol officer</u> is her ideal job. *Subject*

17c. Using the guidelines above, classify the gerunds and progressive verbs in the underlined portions of these sentences:

1. Breathing very cold air can be painful. *Gerund*
2. I love baking cookies. *Gerund*
3. He found much joy in singing. *Gerund*
4. He was singing all the time. *Progressive tense verb*
5. You learn a lot from reading books. *Gerund*
6. When you are driving, time passes quickly. *Progressive tense verb*

17d. Do the same thing in the following sentences, in which the gerunds and progressive-tense verbs are not marked for you:

1. He made a career of programming computers. *Gerund*
2. I was programming computers. *Progressive tense verb*
3. Programming is my job. *Gerund*
4. I love juggling. *Gerund*
5. I am juggling all the time. *Progressive tense verb*
6. Juggling is what I love to do. *Gerund*
7. Once my hobby was juggling. *Gerund*

17e. Using the guidelines above, classify the underlined portions of these sentences as participles, as perfect tense verbs, or as progressive tense verbs.

1. Bob was sleeping for hours. *Progressive tense verb*
2. Bob, driven to exhaustion, had to rest. *Participle*
3. Martha has driven Bob to work all week. *Perfect tense verb*
4. Swimming laps, Bob begins his day briskly. *Participle*
5. Bob, biking for miles, was exhausted. *Participle*
6. Exhausted, Bob nevertheless became intrigued. *Participle* and *participle*
7. Driving to work, Martha saw a red fox. *Participle*

17f. Do the same thing in the following sentences, in which the participles and verbs are not marked for you:

1. <u>Snoring loudly</u>, Susan slept through her history class. *Participle*
2. Susan <u>was snoring</u> loudly in Calculus. *Progressive-tense verb*
3. <u>Driven mad by the noise</u>, Claude threw everything in sight. *Participle*
4. Claude <u>had</u> not <u>slept</u> for two days. *Perfect-tense verb*
5. Claude appeared <u>worn and worried</u>. *Participle and participle*
6. <u>Playing the sax</u>, Al woke up the neighbors. *Participle*
7. <u>Written for Susan</u>, the instructions ordered her to drop her history class. *Participle*

17g. Using the guidelines discussed in this chapter, classify the underlined portions of the following sentences as gerunds, as participles, as perfect-tense verbs, or as progressive tense verbs.

1. His hobby is <u>reading Shakespeare</u>. *Gerund*
2. He <u>is</u> always <u>reading</u> Shakespeare. *Progressive tense verb*
3. <u>Reading Shakespeare aloud</u>, he entranced the audience. *Participle.*
4. Alicia, <u>reading Shakespeare</u>, ignored the speaker. *Participle*
5. <u>Driving at night</u> can be dangerous. *Gerund*
6. I don't like <u>driving at night</u>. *Gerund*
7. <u>Driving late at night</u>, Ed was exhausted. *Participle*
8. <u>Exhausted</u>, Ed drove on. *Participle*
9. Ed <u>was driving</u> three nights a week. *Progressive tense verb*
10. He <u>has exhausted</u> himself with the <u>driving</u>. *Perfect tense verb*

17h. In these sentences, the gerunds, participles, and verbs are not marked for you. Locate and classify the gerunds, participles, perfect tense verbs, and progressive tense verbs:

1. <u>Seen through the window</u>, the room was a mess. *Participle*
2. We <u>have seen</u> the traffic through the window. *Perfect tense verb*
3. My hobby is <u>playing the tuba</u>. *Gerund*
4. Bob <u>is playing</u> the tuba. *Progressive tense verb*
5. <u>Playing the tuba</u>, Bob disturbed the library patrons. *Participle*
6. <u>Feeling sick</u>, Gloria went home. *Participle*
7. Gloria <u>was feeling</u> sick. *Progressive tense verb*
8. Her remarks were about <u>reading Poe</u>. *Gerund*
9. <u>Sailing on the lake</u> is Cal's hobby. *Gerund*
10. I like <u>sailing on the lake</u>. *Gerund*
11. I <u>am sailing</u> again this summer. *Progressive tense verb*

CHAPTER 18

18a. Identify the function of the nominal infinitives in these sentences:

1. <u>To become a star</u> was her adolescent dream. *Subject*
2. She wants <u>to become a star</u>. *Direct object*
3. Her dream, <u>to become a star</u>, may never come true. *Appositive*
4. <u>To live</u> is <u>to dream</u>. *Subject* and *predicate nominative*
5. <u>To know him</u> is <u>to love him</u>. *Subject* and *predicate nominative*
6. I'd like <u>him to do the project</u>. *Direct object*
7. He'll ask <u>her to help</u>. *Direct object*
8. I'm hoping for <u>them to succeed</u>. *Object of a preposition*

18b. Locate the nominal infinitive phrases in these sentences and identify their functions:

1. I need <u>to get some water</u>. *Direct object*

2. <u>To succeed</u> requires hard work. *Subject*
3. <u>To discipline yourself</u> means <u>to make sacrifices</u>. *Subject and predicate nominative*
4. He explained his goal, <u>to become fluent in German</u>. *Appositive*
5. He wants <u>to see me</u> in the morning. *Direct object*
6. It won't be hard for <u>him to see me then</u>. *Object of a preposition*
7. Would you like <u>to see me</u>, too? *Direct object*
8. There's time for <u>me to see you</u>. *Object of a preposition*

18c. Identify the functions of the adjectival infinitives in these sentences: What words do they modify?

1. I have the tools <u>to get the job done</u>. [Modifies *tools*]
2. Time <u>to use the tools</u> is what I need now. [Modifies *Time*]
3. Something <u>to open the tool packages</u> would be handy now. [Modifies *Something*]
4. A scissors <u>to open this</u> would be helpful. [Modifies *scissors*]
5. I could help if I had some dynamite <u>to open this</u>. [Modifies *dynamite*]
6. I need a screwdriver <u>to loosen this</u>. [Modifies *screwdriver*]
7. A screwdriver <u>to loosen this</u> would help. [Modifies *screwdriver*]
8. The tool I need, a screwdriver <u>to loosen this</u>, is not here. [Modifies *screwdriver*]

18d. Locate the adjectival infinitives in these sentences and identify the words they modify:

1. Every day we send letters, urgent messages <u>to complain about the service</u>. [Modifies *messages*]
2. She bought me a carry-on bag <u>to take on my trip</u>. [Modifies *bag*]

3. Someone <u>to guide me on the way</u> would be helpful. [Modifies *someone*]
4. I found someone <u>to guide you</u>. [Modifies *someone*]
5. To relax, he needed a book <u>to interest him</u>. [Modifies *book*]
6. All she asked for was a book <u>to read</u>, a place in which <u>to stay warm</u>, and something <u>to eat</u>. [Modifies, in order, *book, which,* and *something*]

18e. Identify the functions of the adverbial infinitives in these sentences: What words do they modify?

1. <u>To relax</u>, he sang. [Modifies *sang*]
2. He read the book <u>to please his daughter</u>. [Modifies *read*]
3. <u>To please his daughter</u>, he read the book. [Modifies *read*]
4. <u>To become a fireman</u>, the young man studied and trained. [Modifies *studied and trained*]
5. The young man studied and trained <u>to become a fireman</u>. [Modifies *studied and trained*]
6. He was eager <u>to become a fireman</u>. [Modifies *eager*]
7. We were happy <u>to help him</u>. [Modifies *happy*]
8. He was careful <u>to speak with me beforehand</u>. [Modifies *careful*]

18f. Yet again, locate the adverbial infinitives here and identify the words they modify:

1. You need a telescope <u>to be an astronomer</u>. [Modifies *need*]
2. He was ready <u>to be an astronomer</u>. [Modifies *ready*]
3. She was determined <u>to be an astronomer</u>. [Modifies *determined*]
4. Eager <u>to play ball</u>, the team waited. [Modifies *eager*]
5. Happy <u>to see her friend</u>, Julie cried. [Modifies *Happy*]
6. <u>Reluctant to go</u>, the children fidgeted. [Modifies *children*]

7. We were sorry to leave. [Modifies *sorry*]
8. She rose to leave. [Modifies *rose*]

18g. Identify all the infinitive phrases, with complements and modifiers, in these sentences and classify them as nominal, adjectival, or adverbial:

1. That child needs me to look after her. [*nominal* and a *direct object*]
2. To succeed, you have to work hard. [*To succeed* is *adverbial*; *to work hard* is a *direct object*]
3. I'm looking for a place to sit down. [*Adjectival,* modifying *place*]
4. To be blunt, I will say that I'm angry at you. [*Adverbial,* modifying *will say*]
5. He is trying to impress his boss. [*Nominal,* and a *direct object*]
6. I am not here to impress anyone. [*Adverbial,* modifying *am*]
7. His reason, to impress his boss, is sufficient. [*Nominal,* and an *appositive*]
8. His goal is to impress his boss. [*nominal* and a *predicate nominative*]
9. We want her to come to the party. [*nominal* and a *direct object*]
10. We hope that she'd like to come to the party. [*nominal* and a *direct object*]

18h. In the following pairs of sentences, read the first sentence and then analyze the underlined verbal phrase in the second, using the first sentence as a clue. Example:

Randolph likes Italian food.
Randolph likes to eat Italian food.

1. He likes mystery novels.
   He likes <u>to read mystery novels</u>. [The *infinitive phrase* is the direct object of *likes*.]

2. He reads them before school.
   He likes <u>reading them before school</u>. [The *gerund phrase* is the direct object of *likes*.]

3. She is quite ready.
   She is ready <u>to sing</u>. [The *infinitive* is an adverbial modifier of *ready*.]

4. She is very happy.
   She is happy <u>to sing</u>. [The *infinitive* is an adverbial modifier of *happy*.]

5. Smiling, the opera star took center stage.
   <u>Singing the aria loudly</u>, the opera star took center stage. [The *participial phrase* modifies *the opera star*.]

6. He annoys us.
   <u>His singing arias at 6 a.m.</u> annoys us. [The *gerund phrase* is the subject of the sentence.]

7. I don't enjoy opera at 6 a.m.
   I don't enjoy <u>listening to opera</u> at 6 a.m. [The *gerund phrase* is the direct object of *enjoy*.]

8. I want music at any time.
   I want <u>to listen to opera</u> at any time. [The *infinitive phrase* is the direct object of *want*.]

18i. Identify the underlined verbals as gerunds, participles, and infinitives. Then identify the function that the verbal performs in each sentence.

1. He likes <u>to read</u>. [*Nominal infinitive; direct object*]
2. He likes <u>reading novels</u>. [*Gerund; direct object*]
3. <u>Running quickly</u>, he soon arrived at home. [*Participle*, modifying the subject *he*]
4. His <u>singing</u> annoyed us. [*Gerund*; the subject of the sentence]
5. <u>Known to the entire community</u>, the mayor is respected. [*Participle*, modifying *mayor*]
6. <u>The silent film star, seen but never recognized</u>, lived in our neighborhood. [*Participle*, modifying *film star*]
7. He wants <u>to earn money</u>. [*Nominal infinitive; direct object*]
8. He writes <u>to learn</u>. [*Adverbial infinitive*, modifying *writes*]
9. They were prepared <u>to fight</u>. [*Adverbial infinitive*, modifying *were prepared*]
10. <u>To succeed</u>, you must be prepared <u>to work hard</u>. [Two *adverbial infinitives*, both modifying *must be prepared*]

CHAPTER 19

19a. We've examined four classes of pronouns in this chapter. Write the names of the four classes and check your list by looking back through the chapter.

The four classes are demonstrative, reflexive, indefinite, and interrogative

19b. Now, for each of the four classes, write as many pronouns as you can remember. Check your lists by looking back and write down those you forgot.

Demonstrative: *That, this, these,* and *those.*

Reflexive: All the *–self* pronouns, like *myself, yourself, himself, herself, itself, ourselves, yourselves, themselves,* and *oneself.*

Indefinite (of any kind): *All, another, any, anybody, anyone, anything, both, each, enough, everybody, everyone, everything, few, less, little, more, much, nobody, no one, nothing, plenty, several, some, somebody, someone, something; one* and *none, either* and *neither.*

Interrogative: *Who, what, which, whom, whose; whoever, whomever, whatever,* and *whichever.*

19c. Write one sentence that contains an example of each of the four classes you listed above. Compare your sentences with the examples in this chapter.

[The following are merely a few examples of sentences you might have written.]

Demonstrative: <u>That</u> chair belongs on <u>this</u> side of the room.
Reflexive: Move the chair <u>yourself</u>.
Indefinite (of any kind): I won't move <u>anything</u>.
Interrogative: <u>Who</u> do you think you are?

19d. Each of the following sentences contains at least one example of the pronouns described in this chapter. Classify each underlined example.

1. <u>What</u> are you doing? *Interrogative*
2. <u>Who</u> wants to know? *Interrogative*
3. <u>That</u> is the dumbest question <u>anyone</u> ever asked. *Demonstrative; indefinite*
4. I <u>myself</u> am going to teach you some manners because you obviously have <u>none</u>. *Reflexive; indefinite*
5. <u>Both</u> of you need to stop <u>this</u> immediately. *Indefinite; demonstrative*
6. I doubt that you can do <u>anything</u> to stop us. *Indefinite*

7. <u>Whatever</u> could you do? *Interrogative*
8. <u>Anybody</u> who tries to stop me is going to get <u>it</u>. *Indefinite; indefinite*
9. Can't <u>someone</u> do <u>something</u> to help me? *Indefinite; indefinite*
10. I've had <u>enough</u> of <u>all</u> of you. *Indefinite; indefinite*

CHAPTER 20

20a. In the following multiple-choice questions, classify the underlined words. You will use some answers more than once; you may not need some answers at all.

A. Expletive
B. Noun of direct address
C. Appositive
D. Subject of the sentence
E. Sentence modifier

1. <u>It</u> was surprising to hear the news. **A**
2. It was surprising <u>to hear the news</u>. **D**
3. <u>It</u> is time to go. **A**
4. Gosh, <u>John</u>, you forgot your shoes. **B**
5. <u>Frankly</u>, John often forgets his shoes. **E**
6. <u>It</u> is amazing that you forgot your shoes. **A**
7. You can speak with Mr. Smith, <u>the principal</u>. **C**
8. <u>Truly,</u> Mr. Smith is a patient man. [Arguably **E**, a sentence modifier, but this could simply be a moveable adverb: *Mr. Smith is truly a patient man.*]

20b. Underline the absolute phrases in the following sentences:

<u>The sun having set</u>, we walked home.
<u>Our faces wet and cold</u>, we arrived at my parents' house.

20c. Now combine the following pairs of sentences into single sentences, rewriting the first sentence as an absolute phrase. <u>Underline</u> the absolute phrase:

Our time was running short. We hurried to the station.
<u>Our time running short</u>, we hurried to the station.

Her suitcase was safely stowed away. June finally relaxed.
<u>Her suitcase safely stowed away</u>, June finally relaxed.

Our last obstacle was overcome. We all relaxed.
<u>Our last obstacle overcome</u>, we all relaxed.

20d. List the five moods of verbs.

Indicative	Conditional
Interrogative	Subjunctive
Imperative	

20e. List the nine modal auxiliaries.

can	could	must
shall	should	may
will	would	might

CHAPTER 21

21a. In the following sentences, place a comma wherever necessary.

1. Stephen Colbert, the irreverent late-night host, often pokes fun at political leaders.
2. Ralph Ellison's only completed novel, *Invisible Man,* won the National Book Award.
3. The rescue workers, exhausted and discouraged, stared at the rubble without speaking.

4. You can go when you are finished**,** or you can stay and ask questions.
5. When you are finished**,** you can go**,** or you can stay and ask questions. [The first comma is optional.]
6. "He has plundered our seas**,** ravaged our coasts**,** burnt our towns**,** and destroyed the lives of our people." (*The Declaration of Independence*.)
7. The long**,** twisting**,** and muddy road led to an abandoned car.
8. That movie**,** which I've seen before**,** is too violent for me.
9. He thought New York City**,** New York**,** was the greatest city on earth.
10. I have been working hard on my writing**,** and I hope to do better in my next English class.
11. November 22**,** 1963**,** is a day most Baby Boomers remember clearly.

21b. Which sentence below is unfair to teenaged drivers?

Restrictive: Teenaged drivers who drive like maniacs should lose their licenses.

Non-restrictive: Teenaged drivers, who drive like maniacs, should lose their licenses.

Probably the second one is unfair, because its punctuation indicates that *all* teenaged drivers drive like maniacs. The first says that *only* those who drive like maniacs should lose their licenses.

Which sentence below is unfair to grammarians?

Restrictive: Grammarians who are always correcting other people's grammar should be thrown out a second-story window.

Non-restrictive: Grammarians, who are always correcting other people's grammar, should be thrown out a second-story window.

Probably *both*, because neither group really deserves to be thrown out a window. (*Really*.) But the second is more unfair, because it indicates that *all* grammarians are always correcting people.

21c. Insert a colon or semi-colon where necessary or correct a mistake.

1. He was fired yesterday; he simply wasn't doing his job.
2. The boss offered only one explanation: he simply wasn't doing his job. [A semi-colon would work here, too.]
3. A main clause contains a subject and a predicate; it can stand alone as a complete sentence. [A colon would work here, too.]
4. A main clause is easy to define: it contains a subject and a predicate and can stand alone as a complete sentence.
5. Some interesting Southern expressions include *tote, y'all,* and *schlimozel*. [The colon after *include* should be deleted.]
6. *Tote, y'all,* and *schlimozel*: I'm not sure those are all Southern expressions.

21d. Correct punctuation in these quotations as necessary.

1. "My mother had a great deal of trouble with me," wrote Mark Twain, "but I think she enjoyed it."
2. Elbert Hubbard wrote, "Your friend is the man who knows all about you and still likes you."
3. "Senator Phogbound has an evasive word for everything," Jones wrote. "When he was caught tapping into his campaign funds, he called it 'a possible error.'"

21e. Add or correct punctuation wherever necessary.

1. When there's a snow day**,** we typically don't have to make it up unless we've had many of them.
2. It's always a relief after you've finished a research paper and turned it in.
3. St. Louis, Missouri, is Charles**'s** home, and he returns there whenever he can. [According to some style guides, *Charles's* should be *Charles'*.]
4. You can write one independent clause, and it's possible to add a second with a coordinating conjunction.
5. This is one independent clause**;** this is another independent clause.
6. These are the steps in the writing process**:** prewriting, drafting, revision, and exhaustion.
7. Because it's my grandmother's home, Atlanta, Georgia, is my favorite city, and Orlando, Florida, which is not that far from Atlanta, is my favorite vacation spot.
8. My Aunt Hepatica still believes that Orson Welles**'s** drama *The War of the Worlds* was real. [According to some style guides, *Welles's* should be *Welles'*.]

Glossary

In these definitions, words in **bold** type indicate terms defined elsewhere in this glossary. For the sake of readability, only selected cross-referenced terms are in bold. *Italics* mark examples; words of particular relevance in these examples are underscored. Chapter references direct you to discussions of the term. For more cross-references, see the index.

Absolute phrase: A noun phrase, often followed by a **participle**, used adjectivally or adverbially: *His projector having failed, the speaker improvised for the audience.* See Ch. 20.

Action verb: A **verb** that indicates action: *run, walk, speak, read, fly,* and *sail* are all action verbs. Some action verbs are not actions in the usual sense: *pause, consider.* Compare **linking verb**. Do not confuse with **active verb**. See Ch. 2.

Active verb: A **transitive verb** in the **active voice**, describing an action performed by the **subject** upon a **direct object**: *The explosion shattered the windows.* Compare **passive verb**. Do not confuse with **action verb**. See Ch. 14.

Active voice: A quality of **transitive verbs**, present when the **subject** of the verb is actively performing an action upon a **direct object**. Transitive verbs and the sentences that contain them can be said to be in the active or the passive voice. Compare **passive verb** and **passive voice**. See Ch. 14.

Adjectival: A term applied to any word, phrase, or clause that functions as an **adjective**. See Ch. 4.

Adjective: A word that modifies a **noun** or **pronoun**: *a small red convertible*. One of the eight **parts of speech**. See Ch. 4.

Adverbial: A term applied to any word, phrase, or clause that functions as an **adverb**. See Ch. 5.

Adverb: A word that modifies a **verb,** an **adjective,** or another adverb. One of the eight **parts of speech**. See Ch. 5.

Antecedent: The **noun** that is placed by a **pronoun**: *George explained why he was late*. See Ch. 7.

Appositive: A **noun phrase** that renames or provides supplemental information about another noun phrase; the appositive usually appears immediately after the noun phrase: *The club expelled that dull fellow, the grammarian*. See Ch. 15.

Articles: The three words *a, an,* and *the,* considered here as a special class of **adjectives**. See Ch. 4.

Auxiliary verb: When a **simple predicate** contains more than one verb, the words before the **main verb** are auxiliary verbs: *I can juggle*. See Ch. 2.

Case: A quality (or **inflection**) of English **pronouns** that indicates the **function** of the pronoun in a sentence. English pronouns can be in the **nominative, objective,** or **possessive** case. Also see **person**. See Ch. 7.

Clause: A unit of language that contains a **subject** and a **predicate**. See **dependent clause** and **independent**

clause. All complete **sentences** contain at least one clause. See Ch. 10.

Common noun: A **noun** that indicates a general class of persons, places, or things, instead of a particular member of that class. They are typically not capitalized. Examples: *city, state, man*. Compare **proper noun**. See Ch. 15.

Comparison: The three forms of many **adjectives** and **adverbs**, reflecting comparative degrees of quality or intensity: The forms are the *positive degree* (*clumsy, careless*), used to describe one person or thing; the *comparative degree* (*clumsier, more careless*), used to compare two; and the *superlative degree* (*clumsiest, most careless*) to compare three or more. See also **regular adjective** and **regular adverb**. See Ch. 4.

Complement: The noun or adjective that follows a **transitive verb** or a **linking verb** and completes the sense of the verb. There are five kinds: the **direct object, indirect object, object complement, predicate adjective**, and **predicate nominative. Nominals** and **adjectivals** can also be complements. See Chs. 8 and 14.

Complete predicate: The **verb** of a **clause**, with all its **complements** and **modifiers**. *Your paternal grandmother, Mrs. Crowder, is a friend of mine*. Compare **complete subject** and **simple predicate**. See Ch. 1.

Complete subject: The **simple subject** of a sentence, with all its modifiers and associated words (like **adjectives, adjectivals**, and **appositives**). *Your paternal grandmother, Mrs. Crowder, is a friend of mine*. Compare **complete predicate** and **simple subject**. See Ch. 1.

Complex sentence: One of four classifications of **sentences** based on grammatical structure, a complex sentence contains only one **independent clause**, and one or more **dependent**

clauses: *If you have never seen a complex sentence, you are reading one right now.* Compare **simple, compound,** and **compound-complex sentences.** See Ch. 10.

Compound pronoun: A two-part **pronoun: personal pronouns** followed by a second element like *–self* (*myself, yourself, yourselves*), or **interrogative pronouns** followed by *–ever* (*whoever, whomever, whatever*). See also **reflexive pronoun.** See Chs. 12 and 19.

Compound sentence: One of four classifications of **sentences** based on grammatical structure, a compound sentence contains two or more **independent clauses**, and no **dependent clauses**; the clauses are joined by one or more **coordinating conjunctions**: *This is an independent clause, and this is another one.* Compare **simple, complex,** and **compound-complex sentences.** See Chs. 9 and 10.

Compound structure: A grammatical structure consisting of two or more grammatically equivalent units of language, joined by **coordinating conjunctions**: <u>Zombies and grammarians</u> *terrify me.* Compare **compound sentence.** See Ch. 9.

Compound-complex sentence: One of four classifications of **sentences** based on grammatical structure, a compound-complex sentence contains two or more **independent clauses** and one or more **dependent clauses**. *If you have never seen a compound-complex sentence, you are reading one right now, and I hope you appreciate it.* Compare **simple, complex,** and **compound sentences.** See Ch. 10.

Conditional mood: One of the **moods** of verbs, the conditional mood expresses (by means of **modal auxiliaries**) necessary, possible, or permitted actions that may be performed at another time: *I <u>could</u> say more about moods, but you <u>would</u> not appreciate it.* See Ch. 20.

Conjunctions: Words (including **coordinating conjunctions** and **subordinating conjunctions**) that connect one unit of language with another. One of the eight **parts of speech**. See Ch. 9.

Conjunctive adverb: An **adverb** that signals a relationship between the idea of its own clause and the idea of a preceding clause: e.g., *therefore, thus, on the contrary,* and many more. Conjunctive adverbs are *not* conjunctions; they do not, by themselves, join clauses. See Ch. 9.

Coordinating conjunction: A class of seven **conjunctions** that join one unit of language with an equivalent unit, to create a **compound structure**, including **compound sentences**. They are also called the *FANBOYS conjunctions*: *for, and, nor, but, or, yet,* and *so.* Compare **correlative coordinating conjunctions** and **subordinating conjunctions**. See Ch. 9.

Correlative coordinating conjunction: A class of **conjunctions**, just four phrases, each consisting of two to four words, that function like **coordinating conjunctions**: They are *either/or, neither/nor, both/and,* and *not only/but also.* See Ch. 9.

Correlative subordinating conjunctions: A sub-class of **subordinate conjunctions** that introduce **subordinate clauses**. See Ch. 9.

Dangling participle: A **participle** that does not clearly or logically modify a nearby noun: <u>Honking wildly</u>, Jerome watched the car careen by. See Ch. 17.

eclarative sentence: A **sentence** that makes a statement of fact (*I can juggle vases*) in contrast to sentences that ask questions, give commands, or make speculations. Compare **interrogative, imperative,** and **exclamatory sentences.** See Introduction and Chs. 1 and 10.

Definite article: The article *the,* used to indicate a definite **noun phrase**, one that is already known to the listener: *Give me the vase now.* See **indefinite article**. See Ch. 4.

Demonstrative pronoun: Four **pronouns** – *this, that, these,* and *those* – that call attention to the **antecedents** in the immediate physical or verbal context: *That is my bicycle.* See Ch. 19.

Dependent clause: A unit of language that contains a **subject** and a **predicate**, but cannot stand by itself as a complete sentence: e. g., *After we went to the concert, we came home.* The **nominal clause,** the **relative clause,** and the **subordinate clause** are all dependent clauses. Compare **independent clause**. See Chs. 9, 10, and 13.

Descriptive grammar: An approach to language that describes the ways language is actually used by speakers, including speakers of non-standard dialects. Descriptive grammar does not make explicit judgements about what is right or wrong in a sentence. See the Introduction.

Direct object: A **complement** for a **transitive verb** that receives the action of the verb: *I can juggle vases.* See Ch. 8.

Eight parts of speech: See **parts of speech**.

Elliptical clause: A **clause** in which one or more grammatically necessary words (e.g., the **subject, auxiliary verbs**, or the **main verb**) are implicit: *Montrose sings as poorly as I [sing].* See Chs. 9 and 20.

Exclamatory sentence: A **sentence**, often grammatically incomplete, that expresses emotion: *What now? What the heck?* See Ch. 10.

Expletive: A term with several possible meanings. In one common usage, it is a profane or impolite word, sometimes represented in more polite written language like this: *What the [expletive deleted]?*

But here we use the term only for the words *it* and *there* when they are used in place of the **complete subject**, which is postponed until later in the clause, perhaps for emphasis or other purposes. In these examples, the complete subject is underlined:

> No expletive: <u>To find a fly is your soup</u> is upsetting.
> With an expletive: **It** is upsetting <u>to find a fly in your soup</u>.
>
> No expletive: Waiter, <u>a fly is in my soup.</u>
> With an expletive: Waiter, **there** is <u>a fly in my soup</u>.

Other variations are possible: *Waiter, there is a [expletive deleted] fly in my soup.* See Chs. 15 and 20.

Form: A word that may perform any of several **functions**, depending on its context: e.g., a particular noun (a form) can function as a **subject**, an **appositive**, a **direct object**, an **indirect object**, an **object of a preposition**, or others. See Chs. 3 and 16.

Fragment sentence: A grammatically incomplete **sentence**. A fragment may lack a **subject** or a **predicate,** or (in writing) it may be a **dependent clause** punctuated like a complete sentence. Although it is usually written in error, a deliberate fragment, used carefully, can be an effective stylistic device. See Ch. 10.

Function: The grammatical role that a word plays in a particular sentence: e.g., a noun (a **form**) can function as a **subject, direct object, indirect object**, or in other ways. See Ch. 16.

Gender: The **inflection** of **pronouns** that reflects the sex of the **antecedent** of the pronoun: In English, the genders of pronouns are masculine, feminine, and neuter, and are present only in the third-person singular **personal pronouns** and in third-person singular **reflexive pronouns**. See Ch. 7.

Gerund: A kind of **verbal**, a **present participle** that is used **nominally**, as in *Juggling is his hobby*. See Ch. 17.

Grammar: A system of rules by which we create and comprehend sentences. See the Introduction.

Imperative mood: The mood of the verb in imperative sentences, in which the subject and auxiliaries are often implicit: *Stop that!* See Ch. 20.

Imperative sentence: A **sentence** that makes a command: *Stop that juggling!* See Ch. 10.

Indefinite article: The articles *a* and *an*, used to introduce a nonspecific **noun phrase**: *Do not give that man a vase*. See **definite article**. See Ch. 4.

Indefinite pronoun: A **pronoun** that is typically without a specific **antecedent**: *Anyone can dance*. See Ch. 19.**Independent clause:** A **clause** that contains a **subject** and **predicate,** and can stand by itself as a complete sentence: e. g., *We went home after the concert*. Sometimes called a main clause, it does not contain a word (like a **subordinating conjunction** or **relative pronoun**) that makes the clause dependent on another clause for grammatical completeness. Compare **dependent clause**. See Ch. 9.

Indicative mood: The **mood** of a verb used in **declarative sentences**. See Ch. 20.

Indirect object: A **complement** of a **transitive verb** that appears between the verb and the **direct object** and in some sense receives the direct object: *We lent him the vases*. See Ch. 8.

Infinitive verb: A **verbal**, consisting of a basic form of a verb, and typically preceded by the **particle** *to:* e.g., *to strive, to seek, to find*. Infinitives can be used nominally, adjectivally, or adverbially. See Chs. 14 and 18.

Inflection: Changes in the **form** of a word that indicate some change in the word's grammatical function. The suffixes in *walks, walked,* and *walking* are inflections. See the Introduction.

Interjection: A phrase that expresses an emotion or serves some social purpose (e.g., greetings, politeness, agreement, or disagreement), but performs no grammatical **function** in the sentence. One of the eight **parts of speech**. See Ch. 16.

Interrogative adverb: The adverbs *when, where, why,* and *how* when used to create a question: *What did the President know, and when did he know it?* See Ch. 5.

Interrogative mood: The **mood** of verbs in **interrogative sentences**. See Ch. 20.

Interrogative pronoun: Pronouns used to ask questions, the answers to which will typically be **nouns**, and the **antecedent** of the pronoun: *What did the President know, and who did he know?* See Ch. 19.

Interrogative sentence: A sentence that asks a question: *Has Mr. Morton left?* They are often characterized by changes to the typical word order of **declarative sentences**, and by use of the *do* **auxiliary**, **interrogative adverbs** or **pronouns**, or tag questions:

>   Did you do that?
>   What did you do?
>   You did that, didn't you?

See Ch. 10.

Intransitive verb: An **action verb** that does not have a **direct object**: *Mr. Morton left an hour ago.* See Ch. 8.

Irregular adjective: An adjective whose **comparison** does not conform to the patterns found in **regular adjectives**: That is, the comparison is created with other inflections besides the *-er* and *-est* suffixes or the adverbs *more* and *most*: e.g., the comparison *good, better, best* is irregular. See Ch. 4.

Irregular adverb: An adverb whose **comparison** does not conform to the patterns found in **regular adverbs**: That is, the comparison is created with other inflections besides the *-er* and *-est* suffixes or the adverbs *more* and *most*. The comparison *badly, worse, worst* is irregular. See Ch. 5.

Irregular plural: A noun whose plural form does not conform to the usual pattern: *men, women, children, octopi,* and *memoranda* are irregular plurals. See Ch. 15.

Irregular verb: A verb whose principal parts do not conform to the pattern of **regular verbs**: *lie, lay, lain* are the principal parts of the irregular verb *to lie* (meaning "to recline"). See Ch. 3.

Linking verb: A **verb** that appears in a **predicate** that describes the **subject** of the sentence. Linking verbs include *seem, become, appear,* and all forms of *be,* and take **predicate adjectives** and **predicate nominatives** as **complements**: *Mr. Lochenhocher appears angry; he is my neighbor.* Compare **action verb**. See Chs. 2 and 8.

Main clause: See **independent clause**.

Main verb: The last **verb** in the **simple predicate** and the word that specifies the action: *I can juggle.* Compare **auxiliary verb**. See Ch. 2.

Modal auxiliaries: Auxiliary **verbs** used to create the **conditional mood**: They are *can, could; shall, should; will, would;* and *must, might,* and *may.* See Ch. 20.

Modifier: A word that modifies the meanings of other words: **Adjectives** modify the meanings of nouns, as **adverbs** modify the meaning of verbs, adjectives, and other adverbs. See Chs. 1, 4, and 5.

Mood: The qualities of **verbs** that are appropriate for declarations, questions, commands, statements of necessity or possibility, and speculations. See **conditional, imperative**, **indicative**, **interrogative**, and **subjunctive mood**. See Ch. 20.

Nominal: A term applied to a word, phrase, or clause that performs the **function** of a **noun**. See Chs. 12 and 13.

Nominalizer: Any of the words *if, that,* and *whether* when used to create a **nominal** clause: *I will know if you begin juggling.* See Chs. 12 and 13.

Nominative case: One of the three **cases** of English **pronouns**, marking those used as the **subject** of a clause: *I, we, he, she,* and *they* are in the nominative case. See Chs. 7 and 8.

Non-restrictive appositive: An **appositive** that is not needed to clarify the meaning of the noun it renames. It is usually enclosed in commas:

My very best friend, Luis, will drive us to the airport.

You have only one very best friend, so *Luis* merely supplements the meaning of *friend.* Compare **restrictive appositive**. See Ch. 15.

Non-restrictive phrase or clause: A structure that modifies a noun but does not *restrict* (or limit) its reference. These structures are usually set off from the noun by commas, as with this non-restrictive relative clause:

> Bring me the rake, <u>which is in the garage</u>.

(There is only one rake, and the relative clause provides supplementary information.) The term is also applied to **appositives.** Compare **restrictive phrase or clause**. See Chs. 11 and 15.

Noun: A word that indicates a person, place, thing, or idea. Most nouns can be singular or plural; all can be modified by **adjectives**. See **common noun** and **proper noun**. See Chs. 2 and 15.

Noun of direct address: A **noun phrase** that names the person addressed in the sentence: *<u>Phineas</u>, you are stopping on my foot! Please welcome, <u>ladies and gentlemen</u>, our next speaker*. See Ch. 15.

Noun phrase: A **noun** and all its modifiers and related structures (like **appositives**): *Birds, the birds,* and *the terrifying birds in Hitchcock's film* are all noun phrases. See Ch. 4.

Object complement: An adjective or noun phrase that follows a **transitive verb** and its **direct object** and describes the direct object in some way: *We have made Donald Trump <u>President</u>. This election is making me <u>jumpy</u>*. See Ch.8.

Objective case: One of the cases of English pronouns, marking those used as a **direct** or **indirect object**, an **object of a preposition**, and some other functions: *me, us, him, her,* and *them* are all in the objective case. Compare **nominative case** and **possessive case**. See Chs. 7 and 8.

Object of a preposition: The **noun phrase** or **pronoun** that typically follows a **preposition** in a **prepositional phrase**:

To Elise, at your service, and *in your face*. Pronouns will be in the **objective case**. See Ch. 6.

Paragraph coherence: The quality of a paragraph that is unified in subject matter and cohesive in the order and content of sentences: All the sentences in the paragraph are clearly on the same topic, all contributing to the point of the paragraph, and each sentence leads logically to the next. I wandered lonely as a cloud that floats on high o'er vales and hills. Thoughtfully used, **pronouns** and **antecedents**, **adverbs**, conjunctions, and **sentence structure** can contribute to coherence. (Do you see why coherence is important?) See Chs. 9 and 14.

Participle: One kind of **verbal**: The **past participle** or **present participle** form of a verb, used **adjectivally**:

> Past participle: Thrilled, Jerome sped down the street in his new car.
>
> Present participle: Honking wildly, Jerome drove his new car to his parents' home.

Compare the **dangling participle**. See Ch. 17.

Particle: As the term is used here, a particle is the first part of an **infinitive verb** (*to rise, to fall*), or the second part of a **phrasal verb** (*write in, write out, pass out, come to*). These particles always *resemble* prepositions, but are *not* prepositions (or adverbs, or any other part of speech). They are considered *part* of the infinitive or phrasal verb. See Chs. 14 and 18.

Parts of speech: The eight categories of words into which all the words in a sentence can (theoretically) be placed: **adjectives, adverbs, conjunctions, nouns, prepositions, pronouns, verbs,** and **interjections**. See Ch. 16.

Passive complements: The **complements** of **passive verbs**, including **direct objects**, **predicate adjectives**, and **predicate nominatives**: *When Mr. Trump was elected President, Mother was given time to recover.* See Ch. 14.

Passive verb: A **transitive verb** in the passive **voice**, creating a sentence in which the **subject** passively receives the action of the **verb**:

> The windows were shattered by the explosion.
> The explosion was caused by unknown circumstances.

Compare **active verb**. See Ch. 14.

Past: The second of the three **principal parts** of any verb, used to create the **past tense**: e.g., *spoke, sang, shouted.* See Ch. 3.

Past participle: The third of the three **principal parts** of any verb, used with the auxiliary *have* to create **perfect tenses**: *have spoken, had sung, will have shouted.* See Ch. 3.

Past tense: The **tense** created with the second of the three **principal parts**, the **past** form: e.g., *Yesterday we spoke, we sang, and we shouted.* See Ch. 3.

Person: A quality of **personal pronouns** and some other pronouns that indicates that a pronoun refers to the speaker (e.g., *I, we, myself* in the first person), to the audience (*you, yourself* in the second person), or to a third party (*he, she, they, themselves* in the third person). Also see **case**. See Ch. 7.

Perfect progressive tense: The verb tense consisting of an **auxiliary** that is some form of *have been* followed by a **main verb** that is a **present participle**: *have been explaining, had been defining, will have been clarifying.* Compare **simple progressive tense**. See Ch. 3.

Perfect tense: The **tenses** created with the **past participle** of a verb, preceded by some form of the auxiliary *have*. These clauses represent the present perfect, past perfect, and future perfect tenses: e.g., *Today we <u>have spoken,</u> earlier we <u>had spoken</u>, and soon we <u>will have spoken</u> again.* See Ch. 3.

Personal pronouns: The most commonly used **pronouns**, they show number, **case, person,** and **gender:** e.g., *I, me, my; you, yours; she, her, hers.* See Ch. 7.

Phrasal prepositions: A single **preposition** consisting of two words: e.g., *according to, because of.* See Ch. 6.

Phrasal verb: A **main verb** consisting of two words, the second of which (called a **particle**) resembles a **preposition**: *call in* (to telephone), *make up* (to reconcile), *take off* (to leave). See Ch. 14,

Phrase: A word or series of words used as a single grammatical unit: e.g., a **noun phrase** or a **prepositional phrase**. See Ch. 4.

Possessive case: One of the three **cases** of English **personal pronouns**, marking those used to indicate ownership: e.g., *my, mine; your, yours; his, her, hers, its;* and *their, theirs.* See Ch. 7.

Predicate: That portion of any **clause** that provides information about the **subject**, describing the subject or indicating the subject's actions.

>Mr. Morton <u>is outrageous</u>.
>Mr. Morton <u>has broken all the vases</u>.

The predicate of any clause contains the **complete verb** of the sentence, as well as the **modifiers** and **complements** of the verb. See **complete predicate** and **simple predicate**. See Ch. 1.

Predicate adjective: A **complement**: An **adjective** or adjectival phrase that follows a **linking verb** and describes the subject: *Ed is late*. See Ch. 8.

Predicate nominative: A **complement**: A noun, a pronoun, or a nominal phrase or clause that follows a **linking verb** and describes the subject: *Ed is the chairman*. Sometimes called a *predicate noun*. See Ch. 8.

Preposition: A word that typically precedes the **object of a preposition** (a **noun phrase** or **pronoun**) to create a **prepositional phrase**, used as an adjectival or adverbial **modifier**: Some common prepositions are *of, in, to, at, with,* and *beside*. See Ch. 6.

Prepositional phrase: A phrase constructed with a **preposition** and an **object of a preposition** to create an adjectival or adverbial **modifier**: *In a hurry, to school, by nine o'clock*. See Ch. 6.

Prescriptive grammar: An approach to language that describes how English should be used to conform to the standard dialect of the language. See the Introduction.

Present participle: The fourth **principal part** of any **verb,** indicated by the *-ing* suffix: *reading, listening, thinking*. As a **main verb**, it is used to create the **simple progressive** and **perfect progressive tenses**. See Ch. 3.

Principal parts: A conventional way of summarizing the forms of a **verb** used to create **tenses**: the **present**, the **past**, and the **past participle**. A fourth, the **present participle**, is sometimes included. See Ch. 3.

Progressive tense: See **simple progressive** and **perfect progressive**.

Pronoun: A word that typically takes the place of a **noun** that appears elsewhere in the context, as in *Mr. Morton broke his own vases.* See **antecedent**. One of the eight **parts of speech**. See Ch. 7.

Pronoun agreement: The condition of a **personal pronoun** when its number and **gender** is consistent with the number and gender of the **antecedent**: *My daughter actually did her homework.* See Ch. 7.

Proper noun: A **noun** that refers to a *specific* person, place, thing, or idea. In English proper nouns are typically capitalized: *Springfield, Illinois, Lincoln.* Compare **common noun**. See Ch. 15.

Reciprocal Pronoun: The pronouns *each other* and *one another.* See Ch. 19.

Reflexive pronoun: A **compound pronoun** made up of a personal pronoun and *–self*, used for emphasis: *I myself saw it happen. Ask Ruthie to do it herself.* In an **active voice** sentence, reflexive pronouns can be used to indicate an action performed *by* the subject of the sentence *upon* the subject: *Mr. Morton hurt himself.* See Ch. 19.

Regular adjective: An adjective whose **comparison** is formed using only the *-er* and *-est* suffixes or the adverbs *more* and *most.* The comparison *silly, sillier, silliest* is regular. Compare **irregular adjective**. See Ch. 4.

Regular adverb: An adverb whose **comparison** is formed using only the *-er* and *-est* suffixes or the adverbs *more* and *most.* The comparison *erratically, more erratically, most erratically* is regular. Compare **irregular adverb**. See Ch. 5.

Regular verb: A verb whose **principal parts** follow a predictable pattern: The **past** and **past participle** forms are identical, and both end in *-d* (or, in a few cases, *-t*). Examples: *juggle, juggled, have juggled.* Compare **irregular verb**. See Ch. 3.

Relative adverb: The adverbs *where* and *when*, used to create relative clauses that modify nouns of place or time: *Lamar, Missouri, is the little town where Harry S. Truman was born. I was born on April 12, the day when Truman was born.* See Ch. 11.

Relative clause: An adjectival **dependent clause** that is joined to another clause by a **relative pronoun** or **relative adverb**: *That is the idiot who broke all my vases. He will not live to see the day when I let him in my house again.* See Chs. 11 and 13.

Relative pronoun: The **pronouns** *who, whom whose, that,* and *which*, which appear at or near the beginning of a **relative clause**, as in this sentence. See Ch. 11.

Restrictive appositive: An **appositive** that restricts (or limits) the meaning of the noun it renames. It is not enclosed in commas:

> My friend Luis will drive us to the airport.

You have many friends, so *Luis* restricts the reference of *friend*. Compare **non-restrictive appositive**. See Ch. 15.

Restrictive phrase or clause: A structure that modifies a noun and *restricts* (or limits) its reference. These structures are usually not set off from the noun by commas, as with this relative clause:

> Bring me the rake that is in the garage.

(Here the situation is that there is *more than one* rake, and the speaker wants a specific one; the relative clause restricts the range of reference of *rake*.) Compare **non-restrictive phrase or clause**. The term *restrictive* is also applied to **appositives**. See Chs. 11 and 15.

Sentence: A unit of language that contains at least one **independent clause**; sentences are the usual focus of grammatical study. See the Introduction and Ch. 10.

Sentence modifier: A phrase or clause that indicates the writer's attitude or intention about the sentence that contains the modifier; they often resemble **adverbs**: *Tragically, we're nowhere near the end of this glossary*. See Ch. 10.

Sentence structure: A term that often refers to the type and number of clauses a sentence contains, classifying it accordingly as **simple, compound, complex,** or **compound-complex**. But the term is also used for other features of a sentence: e.g., *parallel structure* or *periodic structure*. See the Introduction and Ch. 10.

Simple predicate: The simple predicate consists only of the **main verb** and its **auxiliary verbs**, excluding any **modifiers** or **complements**. In the preceding sentence, the simple predicate is *consists*. See Ch. 1.

Simple progressive tense: Also called the **progressive** tense. The verb tense consisting of an **auxiliary** that is some form of *be* followed by a **main verb** that is a **present participle**: *am explaining, was defining, will be clarifying*. Compare **perfect progressive tense**. See Ch. 3.

Simple sentence: A **sentence** consisting of just one **independent clause** and no **dependent clauses**: *Mr. Morton juggles*. See also **compound, complex,** and **compound-complex sentences**. See Ch. 10.

Simple subject: The **noun phrase** or **pronoun** that indicates what (or whom) the clause is about, excluding modifiers or other associated structures: *Little <u>Ruthie</u>, the girl next door, is learning the bagpipes. The <u>girl</u> next door, that Ruthie, is driving me crazy.* See **complete subject** and **predicate**. See Ch. 1.

Simple tenses: The past, present, and future **tenses** of a verb, in contrast to the **perfect** and **progressive** tenses: *I juggle; I juggled, I will juggle.* See Ch. 3.

Subject: That portion of any **clause** that states what the clause is about:

<u>Mr. Morton</u> is outrageous.
<u>Mr. Morton</u> has broken all the vases.

The **complete subject** of any clause typically contains a noun or pronoun (or some nominal structure) as well as **modifiers** of the noun. See **complete subject** and **simple subject**. See Ch. 1.

Subject complement: Another common term for the **predicate adjective** and **predicate nominative**.

Subject-verb agreement: The condition of a verb when it is consistent with the number and person of the subject of the verb: *I juggle, he juggles, they juggle.* See Ch. 2.

Subjunctive mood: The **mood** of verbs in clauses about hypothetical situations (e.g., wishes, prayers, and speculations), often combined with **conditional mood** clause: *If I <u>were</u> you, I'd stop juggling.* See Ch. 20.

Subordinate clause: An adverbial **dependent clause** that begins with a **subordinating conjunction**. *<u>Before Ruthie took up the bagpipes</u>, Mr. Lochenhocher was a happy man.* See Chs. 9 and 13.

Subordinating conjunction: A class of **conjunctions** that join an independent clause with a **dependent clause** to create a **complex** or **compound-complex sentence.** Compare **coordinating conjunction** and **subordinate clause.** See Ch. 9.

Tag Question: A tag question is added to the end of a **declarative sentence** with a comma, and it repeats the **auxiliary verb** and the subject of the declarative. If the declarative is positive (*You did forget your textbooks*), the tag question is negative (*didn't you?*). If the declarative is negative (*I won't need them*), the tag is positive (*will I?*). See Ch. 10.

Tense: The quality of **verbs,** signaled by **inflections** and **auxiliaries,** that indicates the point in time when the action took place: e.g., past, present, or future. See **simple**, **perfect**, and **progressive tenses**. See Ch. 3.

Three principal parts: See **principal** parts, and Ch. 3.

Transitive verb: A **verb** that is performing an action upon a **direct object** in an **active voice** sentence, or performing an action upon the **subject** in a **passive voice** sentence. See Ch. 8.

Transposed order: Describes a **declarative sentence** in which the **subject** appears *after* the **predicate:** *Quietly rose the sun. Gently fell the vases.* See Ch. 1.

Verb: One of the eight **parts of speech**, verbs indicate actions (e.g., *read, write, walk, drive, think, consider*) or states of being (e.g., *become, seem,* and forms of *be*). Verbs are often said to be the most important part of the sentence because they contain so much information (e.g., **tense, voice, mood,** as well as the state of being or action expressed in the **main verb**), and because they are a locus for other important structures (**adverbials** and **complements**). See Chs. 2, 3, 8, and 14.

Verbal: A verb **form** used for another **function,** as a noun, adjective, or adverb. There are three kinds: the **gerund, infinitive,** and **participle.** See Chs. 17 and 18.

Voice: A term applied to **transitive verbs** and the sentences that contain them: These verbs and sentences are said to be *in* the **active voice** or the **passive voice**, depending on the expressed relationship between the subject of the sentence and its verb: Is the subject *actively* performing the action (<u>Mr. Morton juggled</u> *the vases*) or *passively* receiving it (<u>The vases were juggled</u> *by Mr. Morton*)? See Ch. 14.

Index

A

adjective 31, 181
  adjectival 34
  article 31
  comparison of 34
  irregular adjective 37
  predicate adjective 82
  regular adjective 35
adverb 12, 41, 181
  adverbial 45
  comparison of 42
  conjunctive adverb 107
  interrogative adverb 46
  irregular adverb 44
  relative adverb 129
article 31
  definite article 32
  indefinite article 32

C

capitalization 246
case x, 67
  nominative case 67, 88
  objective case 68, 84, 85, 87
  possessive case 68
clause 93, 113

dependent clause 101, 113, 147
elliptical clause 102
independent clause 101, 113
nominal clause 114, 133, 140, 148, 172
relative clause 114, 126, 148, 182
  non-restrictive 132, 238
  restrictive 132
subordinate clause 96, 147, 182
conjunction 91, 181
conjunctive adverb 107
coordinating conjunction 91
correlative coordinating conjunction 95
correlative subordinating conjunction 99
subordinating conjunction 96

E

expletive 173
expletive *it* 221
expletive *there* 221

F

form 182
function 182

G

grammar v
descriptive grammar x
generative grammar ix
prescriptive grammar x
traditional grammar ix

I

inflection vi
interjection 181

M

modifier 2, 30
sentence modifier 223
mood 225
conditional mood 226
imperative mood 226

indicative mood 226
interrogative mood 226
subjunctive mood 229

N

noun 6, 168, 181
  common noun 168
  direct object viii, 83
  indirect object viii, 84
  irregular plural 169
  nominalizer 142, 148
  noun phrase 30
  of direct address 175
  proper noun 168
  question-word nominal 141

P

paragraph coherence 107, 121
particle 54, 163, 183
parts of speech 180
  adjective 31, 181
  adverb 12, 41, 181
  conjunction 91, 181
  interjection 179, 181
  noun 6, 168, 181
  preposition 52, 100, 181
  pronoun 31, 65, 181
  verb 7, 181
phrase 30
  absolute phrase 224
predicate ix, 1
  complement (of verb) 81
  complete predicate 2
  object complement 86
  passive complement 160
  predicate adjective 57
  predicate nominative 82
  simple predicate 2
preposition 52, 100, 181
  object of 52
  phrasal preposition 59
  prepositional phrase 52, 159, 163

pronoun 31, 65, 181
  agreement of 73
  antecedent 65
  appositive 171
    non-restrictive appositive 177
    restrictive appositive 177
  compound pronoun 141, 216
  demonstrative pronoun 213
  gender of 67
  indefinite pronoun 215
  intensifying pronoun 213
  interrogative pronoun 46, 214
  personal pronoun 66, 212
  person (of pronoun) 67
  reciprocal pronoun 217
  reflexive pronoun 87, 212
  relative pronoun 126, 212
punctuation 233
  abbreviation 246
  apostrophe 234
  colon 240
  comma 235
    parenthetical commas 132, 235
    serial commas 238
    single comma 236
  ellipses 244
  period 246
  quotation marks 242
  semi-colon 239
  square brackets 244

S

sentence viii, 114
  complex sentence 116
  compound-complex sentence 116
  compound sentence 93, 115
  compound structure 91
  declarative sentence viii, 1, 117
  exclamatory sentence 119
  fragment 116
  imperative sentence 119
  interrogative sentence 117

simple sentence viii, 115
transposed order 4
subject ix, 1
  complete subject 2
  simple subject 2
  subject-verb agreement 12

T

tag question 118
tense x, 16
  perfect progressive tense 20
  perfect tense 18
  simple progressive tense 19
  simple tense 17
transposed order 4

V

verb 7, 181
  action verb 7
  active verb vii
  active voice verb 159, 161
  auxiliary verb 10
    modal auxiliary 11, 226
      ought to 228
  complement of 160
    passive complement 160
  complement (of verb) 81
  infinitive 162, 197
    bare infinitive 201
    passive infinitive 202
    perfect infinitive 203
  intransitive verb 24, 83, 158
  irregular verb 22
  linking verb 7
  main verb 9
  participle 54, 58, 188
  passive verb vii
  passive voice verb 159, 161, 164
  past participle 18, 21, 159
  phrasal verb 54, 163
  present participle 21
  principal parts of 16, 21

regular verb 16, 21
  subject-verb agreement 12
  transitive verb 24, 83, 158
  verbal 185, 197
  voice of 158
verbal 185, 197
  gerund 185
  infinitive 162, 185
    dangling infinitive 205
  participle 54, 58, 185, 188
    dangling participle 189
voice 158
  active voice 159, 164
  passive voice 159, 164

www.ingramcontent.com/pod-product-compliance
Lightning Source LLC
Chambersburg PA
CBHW041312240426
43669CB00023B/2963